CIMA Exam Practice Kit

E2 – Enterprise Management

CIMA Exam Practice Kit

E2 – Enterprise Management

Nick Best
Charlie Dalton

Amsterdam • Boston • Heidelberg • London • New York • Oxford
Paris • San Diego • San Francisco • Singapore • Sydney • Tokyo

CIMA Publishing
An imprint of Elsevier
Linacre House, Jordan Hill, Oxford OX2 8DP
30 Corporate Drive, Burlington, MA 01803

First published 2008

Copyright © 2009, Elsevier Ltd. All rights reserved

No part of this publication may be reproduced in any material form (including photocopying or storing in any medium by electronic means and whether or not transiently or incidentally to some other use of this publication) without the written permission of the copyright holder except in accordance with the provisions of the Copyright, Designs and Patents Act 1988 or under the terms of a licence issued by the Copyright Licensing Agency Ltd, 90 Tottenham Court Road, London, England W1T 4LP. Applications for the copyright holder's written permission to reproduce any part of this publication should be addressed to the publisher

Permissions may be sought directly from Elsevier's Science and Technology Rights Department in Oxford, UK: phone: (+44)-(0) 1865 843830; fax: (+44)-(0) 1865 853333; e-mail: permissions@elsevier.com. You may also complete your request on-line via the Elsevier homepage (http://www.elsevier.com), by selecting 'Customer Support' and then 'Obtaining Permissions'

Notice
No responsibility is assumed by the publisher for any injury and/or damage to persons or property as a matter of products liability, negligence or otherwise, or from any use or operation of any methods, products, instructions or ideas contained in the material herein.

British Library Cataloguing in Publication Data
A catalogue record for this book is available from the British Library

Library of Congress Cataloguing in Publication Data
A catalogue record for this book is available from the Library of Congress

978-1-85617-735-1

For information on all CIMA Publishing Publications
visit our website at www.cimapublishing.com

Typeset by Macmillan Publishing Solutions (www.macmillansolutions.com)

Printed and bound in Great Britain

09 10 11   11 10 9 8 7 6 5 4 3 2 1

Working together to grow
libraries in developing countries

www.elsevier.com | www.bookaid.org | www.sabre.org

ELSEVIER   BOOK AID International   Sabre Foundation

Contents

Syllabus Guidance, Learning Objectives and Verbs	xi
Learning Outcomes, Syllabus Content and Examintaion Format	xv
Examination Techniques	xxi

1 Business Strategy — 1
- Business strategy — 3
- Levels of strategy — 3
- Corporate strategy — 3
  - Business strategy — 3
  - Functional/operational strategies — 4
- Rational planning approach to strategy formulation — 4
  - Advantages of the rational approach — 5
  - Disadvantages of planned strategies — 5
  - Typical usage — 5
- The resource-based view of strategy — 5
- The ecological perspective on the firm – The adaptive or evolutionary approach to strategy — 6
- The emergent strategy approach to strategy formulation (Mintzberg) — 6
- Logical incrementalism — 6
- System-based views on strategy (Mintzberg) — 7
- Knowledge test – Quick questions — 7
- Knowledge test – Answers — 9

2 Assessing the External Environment — 11
- Political/legal — 13
- Economic — 13
- Social — 13
- Technical — 14
- Examining industry profitability – Porter's five forces — 14
- Competitors — 15
- Threat of new entrants — 15
- Buyer power — 15
- Supplier power — 15
- Substitute products — 15
- Porter's Diamond – The competitive of a nation's industries — 15
  - Factor conditions — 16

v

	Demand conditions	16
	Related and supporting industries	16
	Firm strategy, structure and rivalry	16
	Interactions between the determinants	16
	Knowledge test – Quick questions	16
	Knowledge test – Answers	17

3 Strategic Models and Tools — 19

Mission — 21
Objectives — 22
    Hierarchy of objectives — 22
    SMART objectives — 22
Stakeholders — 23
    Mendelow's power/interest matrix — 23
Corporate appraisal – SWOT analysis — 24
The level of decision-making — 24
    Centralisation — 24
    Advantages — 24
    Decentralisation — 25
    Advantages — 25
    The value chain — 25
    Primary activities — 26
    Support activities — 26
    The finance function's role in adding value — 26
Porter's generic strategies — 27
    Cost leadership — 27
    Differentiation — 27
    Focus — 27
    Being "stuck in the middle" — 28
Knowledge test – Quick questions — 28
Knowledge test – Answers — 29

4 Organisational Culture, Ethics and Governance — 33

Culture — 35
    Influences on culture — 35
    Importance of culture — 36
    Cultural control — 36
Cultural models — 36
    Handy — 36
Ethics and social responsibility — 37
Why are they important? — 37
    Ethical control — 37
    CIMA code of ethics — 38
Corporate governance — 39
    Encouraging innovation and creativity — 39
    Benefits — 40
    Drawbacks — 40
Knowledge test – Quick questions — 40
Knowledge test – Answers — 42

5 Introduction to Project Management — 43
- Projects and project management — 45
  - Projects — 45
  - Project management — 45
  - Objectives of project management — 46
  - Contrast with line management — 47
  - Programme management — 47
- Stakeholders — 47
  - Project stakeholders — 47
  - Project managers — 48
  - The project team — 48
  - Project team structure — 49
  - Organisational structure and the link to project success — 49
- Knowledge test – Quick questions — 49
- Knowledge test – Answers — 52

6 The Project Management Process — 55
- The project life cycle – the 4-D model — 57
  - Define the project — 57
  - Design the project — 57
  - Deliver the project — 58
  - Develop the process — 58
- PRINCE 2 — 58
  - Implications for project staff of PRINCE 2 — 60
- Maylor's 7-S model — 60
- Knowledge test – Quick questions — 61
- Knowledge test – Answers — 63

7 Project Planning — 65
- Project plans — 67
  - The time/cost/quality trade-off — 67
  - Project scope — 68
  - Risk management — 68
- Evaluating plans — 68
- Project planning tools — 70
  - Work breakdown structure — 70
  - Network analysis — 70
- Notation and rules for drawing a network diagram — 71
  - Example of a network diagram — 73
  - Gantt charts — 73
  - Resource histograms — 74
  - Gates and milestones — 75
- Dealing with uncertainty — 75
  - PERT (Project Evaluation and Review Technique) — 75
  - Scenario planning — 75
  - Buffering — 76
- Project management software — 76
- Knowledge test – Quick questions — 76
- Knowledge test – Answers — 79

8 Executing and Completing Projects — 81
- Allowing for change during a project — 83
- Controlling performance — 83
  - Project not meeting objectives — 83
  - Performance management — 84
  - Conformance management — 84
  - Earned value management — 84
- Project completion — 85
  - Completion activities — 85
  - Post completion review/audit — 85
- Project documentation — 86
  - Project initiation document/project charter/project brief — 86
  - Project quality plan — 86
  - Business case — 86
  - Project plan — 86
  - Progress reports — 86
  - Completion report — 87
- Knowledge test – Quick questions — 87
- Knowledge test – Answers — 89

9 Introduction to Management Theory Leadership — 91
- Power — 93
- Authority — 93
- Responsibility — 93
- Delegation — 93
- Leadership — 94
  - Personality trait theories — 94
  - Characteristics of managers and entrepreneurs — 94
  - Management styles — 94
  - Contingency theories of leadership — 95
  - Bureaucracy (late nineteenth century and early twentieth century) — 95
- Knowledge test – Quick questions — 95
- Knowledge test – Answers — 96

10 The Management of Groups — 99
- Behaviour in work groups — 101
  - Informal groups — 101
  - Formal — 101
  - Teams — 101
  - Formation of groups — 102
  - Roles within the team — 102
- Communication — 102
  - The role of communication in organisations — 102
  - Communication methods – oral and written — 103
  - Communication methods – meetings — 103
  - Roles of team members within meetings — 103
- Negotiation — 103
  - Characteristics of negotiations — 104
  - Stages of negotiations — 104
  - Motivating group members — 104

	Knowledge test – Quick questions	105
	Knowledge test – Answers	107
11	**Control, Conflict and Discipline**	**109**
	Internal control systems	111
	Levels of control	111
	Managing individuals	112
	Legal issues	112
	Health and safety	112
	Diversity and equal opportunities	113
	Conflict in organisations	114
	Symptoms	114
	Sources of conflict	114
	Conflict handling strategies	114
	Discipline	115
	Disciplinary procedures	115
	Disciplinary sanctions	115
	ACAS code of practice	115
	Knowledge test – Quick questions	116
	Knowledge test – Answers	118
12	**Question Bank**	**121**
	Questions 1–5 Strategic management	123
	Questions 8–10 Project management	125
	Questions 14–19 Management of relationships	127
	Scenario 1 – Strategic management (Questions 20–22)	130
	Scenario 2 – Project management (Questions 23–25)	132
	Scenario 3 – Management of relationships (Questions 26–28)	135
13	**Solutions**	**139**
	Answers to questions 1-5 Strategic management	141
	Answers to questions 8-10 Project management	146
	Answers to questions 15–18 Management of relationships	154
	Scenario-based answers	157
	Scenario 1 – Strategic management (Answers to questions 20-22)	157
	Scenario 2 – Project management (Answers to questions 23-25)	162
	Scenario 3 – Management of relationships (Answers to questions 26-28)	168
14	**Mock Exam and Solutions**	**181**
	Mock Exam Paper	183
	Section A	183
	Section B	185
	Mock Exam Solutions	187
	Solutions to Section A	187
	Solutions to Section B	190
Exam Q & As		**197**

Syllabus Guidance, Learning Objectives and Verbs

A The Syllabus

The syllabus for the CIMA Professional Chartered Management Accounting qualification 2010 comprises three learning pillars:

- Enterprise pillar
- Financial pillar
- Operational pillar

Subjects within each learning pillar of the qualification are set at three levels, Operational level, Managerial level and Strategic level. The pass mark is 50%.

For further syllabus information please see CIMA's website www.cimaglobal.com.

B Aims of the Syllabus

The aims of the syllabus for the CIMA Professional Chartered Management Accounting qualification 2010 are:

- To provide for the Institute, an adequate basis for assuring society that those admitted to membership are competent to act as management accountants for entities, whether in manufacturing, commercial or service organisations, in the public or private sectors of the economy.
- To enable the Institute to examine whether prospective members have an adequate knowledge, understanding and mastery of the stated body of knowledge and skills.
- To enable the Institute to assess whether prospective members have completed initial professional development and acquired the necessary work based practical experience and skills.

C Study Weightings

Within a syllabus subject, a percentage weighting is shown against each section topic and is intended as a guide to the proportion of study time each topic requires.

xii Syllabus Guidance, Learning Objectives and Verbs

It is essential that all topics in the syllabus are studied, since any single examination question may examine more than one topic, or carry a higher proportion of marks than the percentage study time suggested.

The weightings *do not* specify the number of marks that will be allocated to topics in the examination.

D Learning Outcomes

Each subject within the three learning pillars of the syllabus is divided into a number of broad syllabus topics. The topics contain one or more lead learning outcomes, related component learning outcomes and indicative knowledge content.

A learning outcome has two main purposes:

(a) to define the skill or ability that a well-prepared candidate should be able to exhibit in the examination;
(b) to demonstrate the approach likely to be taken by examiners in examination questions.

The learning outcomes are part of a hierarchy of learning objectives. The verbs used at the beginning of each learning outcome relate to a specific learning objective e.g.

> *Evaluate* performance using fixed and flexible budget reports

The verb **'*evaluate*'** indicates a high, level 5, learning objective. Because learning objectives are hierarchical, it is expected that at this level, students will have knowledge of fixed and flexible budget techniques, to be able to apply them and assess performance using relevant reports.

The following table lists the learning objectives and the verbs that appear in the syllabus learning outcomes and examination questions:

	Learning Objective	Verbs Used	Definition
1	Knowledge *What you are expected to know*	List State Define	Make a list of Express, fully or clearly, the details/facts of Give the exact meaning of
2	Comprehension *What you are expected to understand*	Describe Distinguish Explain Identify Illustrate	Communicate the key features of Highlight the differences between Make clear or intelligible/state the meaning or purpose of Recognise, establish or select after consideration Use an example to describe or explain something
3	Application *How you are expected to apply your knowledge*	Apply Calculate Demonstrate Prepare Reconcile Solve Tabulate	Put to practical use Ascertain or reckon mathematically Prove with certainty or exhibit by practical means Make or get ready for use Make or prove consistent/compatible Find an answer to Arrange in a table

4	Analysis *How you are expected to analyse the detail of what you have learned*	Analyse Categorise Compare and contrast Construct Discuss Interpret Prioritise Produce	Examine in detail the structure of Place into a defined class or division Show the similarities and/or differences between Build up or compile Examine in detail by argument Translate into intelligible or familiar terms Place in order of priority or sequence for action Create or bring into existence
5	Evaluation *How you are expected to use your learning to evaluate, make decisions or recommendations*	Advise Evaluate Recommend	Counsel, inform or notify Appraise or assess the value of Pro pose a course of action

E Study Weightings

Within a syllabus subject, a percentage weighting is shown against each section topic and is intended as a guide to the proportion of study time each topic requires.

It is essential that all topics in the syllabus are studied, since any single examination question may examine more than one topic, or carry a higher proportion of marks than the percentage study time suggested.

The weightings *do not* specify the number of marks that will be allocated to topics in the examination.

Learning Outcomes, Syllabus Content and Examination Format

Paper E3 – Enterprise Strategy

Syllabus Overview

Paper E3 continues the integration of skills across functions, but concentrates on developing the knowledge and skills used in designing and implementing strategy. Strategy is developed in a context, and understanding how the organisation's external environment and stakeholders affect strategy development is important. Context and the internal capabilities of the organisation shape the generation and evaluation of strategic options. Implementing strategy involves tools and techniques associated with change management. Finally, the paper requires the application of tools to assist in the evaluation of the performance implications of a given strategy.

Syllabus Structure

The syllabus comprises the following topics and study weightings:

A	Interacting with the Competitive Environment	20%
B	Change Management	20%
C	Evaluation of Strategic Options	30%
D	Implementation of Strategic Plans	30%

Assessment Strategy

There will be a written examination paper of 3 hours, plus 20 minutes of pre-examination question paper reading time. The examination paper will have the following sections:

Section A – 50 marks

A maximum of four compulsory questions, totalling 50 marks, all relating to a pre-seen case study and further new unseen case material provided within the examination. (Note: The pre-seen case study is common to all three of the Strategic level papers at each examination sitting i.e. paper E3, P3 and F3.)

Section B – 50 marks

Two questions, from a choice of three, each worth 25 marks. Short scenarios will be given, to which some or all questions relate.

Learning Outcomes and Syllabus Content

E3 – A. Interacting with the Competitive Environment (20%)

Learning Outcomes		Content
Lead	Component	
1. Evaluate the key external factors affecting an organisation's strategy. (5)	(a) Evaluate the impact and influence of the external environment on an organisation and its strategy. (b) Recommend approaches to business/government relations and to relations with civil society. (c) Discuss the drivers of external demands for corporate social responsibility and the firm's response. (d) Recommend how to manage relationships with stakeholders. (e) Recommend how to interact with suppliers and customers.	• Non-market strategy and forms of corporate political activity. (A, B) • External demands for responsible business practices and ways to respond to these. (A, C) • Stakeholder management (stakeholders to include government and regulatory agencies, non-governmental organisations and civil society, industry associations, customers and suppliers). (C, D) • The customer portfolio: Customer analysis and behaviour, including the marketing audit and customer profitability analysis as well as customer retention and loyalty. (E) • Strategic supply chain management. (E) • Implications of these interactions for Chartered Management Accountants and the management accounting system. (B, C, D, E)
2. Evaluate the impact of information systems on an organisation. (5)	(a) Evaluate the impact of the Internet on an organisation and its strategy. (b) Evaluate the strategic and competitive impact of information systems.	• The impact of IT (including the Internet) on an organisation (utilising frameworks such as Porter's Five Forces, the Value Chain). (A, B) • Competing through exploiting information (rather than technology), e.g. use of databases to identify potential customers or market segments, and the management of data (warehousing and mining). (A, B) • Contemporary developments in the commercial use of the Internet (e.g. Web 2.0) (A, B)

E3 – B. Change Management (20%)

Learning Outcomes		Content
Lead	**Component**	
1. Advise on important elements in the change process. (5)	(a) Discuss the concept of organisational change. (b) Recommend techniques to manage resistance to change.	• External and internal change triggers (e.g. environmental factors, mergers and acquisitions, re-organisation and rationalisation). (A, B) • Stage models of change. (A, B) • Problem identification as a precursor to change. (A, B) • Cultural processes of change i.e. change within the context of the whole firm. (B)
2. Evaluate tools and methods for successfully implementing a change programme. (5)	(a) Evaluate approaches to managing change. (b) Compare and contrast continuous and discontinuous change. (c) Evaluate tools, techniques and strategies for managing the change process. (d) Evaluate the role of leadership in managing the change process.	• The importance of managing critical periods of discontinuous change. (A) • Tools, techniques and models associated with organisational change. (C, D) • Approaches, styles and strategies of change management. (C, D) • Importance of adaptation and continuous change. (A, B) • Leading change. (D)
3. Recommend change management processes in support of strategy implementation. (5)	(a) Evaluate the role of change management in the context of strategy implementation. (b) Evaluate ethical issues and their resolution in the context of organisational change.	• Change management and its role in the successful implementation of strategy. (A) • The advantages and disadvantages of different styles of management on the successful implementation of strategy. (A) • Group formation within organisation and its impact on change processes within organisations. (A) • Business ethics in general and the CIMA Code of Ethics for Professional Accountants (Parts A and B) in the context of implementation of strategic plans. (B)

E3 – C. Evaluation of Strategic Position and Strategic Options (30%)

Lead	Learning Outcomes	Content
	Component	
1. Evaluate the process of strategy development. (5)	(a) Evaluate the process of strategy formulation. (b) Evaluate strategic options. (c) Evaluate different organisational structures. (d) Discuss the role and responsibilities of directors in the strategy development process.	• Mission statements and their use in orientating the organisation's strategy. (A) • The process of strategy formulation. (A) • The identification and evaluation of strategic options. (B) • Strategic options generation (e.g. using Ansoff's product/market matrix and Porter's generic strategies). (B) • Real Options as a tool for strategic analysis. Note: Complex numerical questions will not be set. (B) • Scenario planning and long-range planning as tools in strategic decision-making. (B) • Game theoretic approaches to strategic planning and decision-making. Note: Complex numerical questions will not be set. (B) • Acquisition, divestment, rationalisation and relocations strategies and their place in the strategic plan. (B, C) • The relationship between strategy and organisational structure. (C) • The role and responsibilities of directors in making strategic decisions (including issues of due diligence, fiduciary responsibilities). (D)
2. Evaluate tools and techniques used in strategy formulation. (5)	(a) Evaluate strategic analysis tools. (b) Recommend appropriate changes to the product portfolio of an organisation to support the organisation's strategic goals. (c) Produce an organisation's value chain. (d) Discuss both qualitative and quantitative techniques in the support of the strategic decision-making function.	• Audit of resources and the analysis of this for use in strategic decision-making. (A) • Forecasting and the various techniques used: trend analysis, system modelling, in-depth consultation with experts (Delphi method). (A) • Management of the product portfolio. (B) • Value chain analysis. (C) • Strategic decision-making processes. (D)

E3 – D. Implementation of Strategic Plans and Performance Evaluation (30%)

Learning Outcomes		Content
Lead	**Component**	
1. Evaluate the tools and processes of strategy implementation.	a) Recommend appropriate control measures. b) Evaluate alternative models of performance measurement. c) Recommend solutions to problems in performance measurement. d) Advise managers on the development of strategies for knowledge management and information systems that support the organisation's strategic requirements. e) Recommend changes to information systems appropriate to the organisation's strategic requirements.	• Alternative models of performance measurement (e.g. the balanced scorecard). (A, B, C) • Business unit performance and appraisal, including transfer pricing, reward systems and incentives. (B) • Project management: monitoring the implementation of plans. (B) • The implementation of lean systems across an organisation. (C) • Theories of control within organisations and types of organisational structure (e.g. matrix, divisional, network). (A, B, C) • Assessing strategic performance (i.e. the use and development of appropriate measures that are sensitive to industry characteristics and environmental factors). (B, C) • Non-financial measures and their interaction with financial ones. (Note: candidates will be expected to use both qualitative and quantitative techniques.) (A, B, C) • The purpose and contents of information systems strategies, and the need for strategy complementary to the corporate and individual business strategies. (D, E) • Critical success factors: links to performance indicators and corporate strategy, and their use as a basis for defining an organisation's information needs. (A, B)

Examination Techniques

Essay questions

Your essay should have a clear structure, that is, an introduction, a middle and an end. Think in terms of 1 mark for each relevant point made.

Numerical questions

It is essential to show workings in your answer. If you come up with the wrong answer and no workings, the examiner cannot award any marks. However, if you get the wrong answer but apply the correct technique then you will be given some marks.

Reports and memorandum

Where you are asked to produce an answer in a report type format you will be given easy marks for style and presentation.

- A *report* is a document from an individual or group in one organisation sent to an individual or group in another.
- A *memorandum* is an informal report going from one individual or group to another individual or group in the same organisation.

You should start a report as follows:

To: J. SMITH, CEO, ABC plc

From: M ACCOUNTANT

Date: 31st December 200X

Terms of Reference: Financial Strategy of ABC plc

Multiple choice questions managerial level

From May 2005 some multiple choice questions will be worth more than two marks. Even if you get answer wrong, you may still get some marks for technique. Therefore show all workings on such questions.

Business Strategy

Business Strategy 1

Business strategy

 A business strategy can be defined as:

"A course of action, including the specification of resources required, to achieve a specific objective" (CIMA official terminology).

This usually involves

- a long-term view
- consideration of the external environment outside the organisation
- matching strategies with internal strengths
- how the organisation will achieve competitive advantage
- resource plans
- how stakeholder needs will be fulfilled.

Levels of strategy

Strategies can be developed at three different levels in organisations.

Corporate strategy

This is for the organisation as a whole and considers

- which business areas to operate in?
- which markets to sell to? financing
- the business meeting shareholder
- needs organisational structure.

Business strategy

Many businesses are structured with many different divisions. Each division is likely to have different competitors, customers, suppliers and other stakeholders, and so a division specific strategy is required. Such divisions are called strategic business units. These business strategies consider

- products and product features
- which markets?
- direct competition and how to be competitive
- marketing approach
- business resources (people, buildings, machinery).

Functional/operational strategies

For each functional or operational area (e.g. IT, R&D, HR, etc.), a strategy is devised to act as a long-term plan which will support the overall strategy of the business unit.

Rational planning approach to strategy formulation

The rational approach provides a step-by-step formal process to the development of a business strategy. It consists of a number of distinct stages:

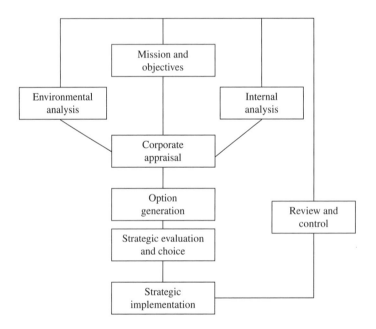

(a) *Mission and objectives.* Defines the business purpose and direction.
(b) *Environmental analysis.* Examines factors external to the organisation, such as political and legal issues, the changing competitive environment and changing customer requirements to determine opportunities and threats.
(c) *Internal analysis.* An examination of the internal resources and competencies to determine the organisation's strengths and weaknesses.
(d) *Corporate appraisal.* A summary of the current position of the organisation, often using a SWOT analysis which summarises the organisation's strengths, weaknesses, opportunities and threats.
(e) *Option generation.* An analysis of possible strategies that will fill the gap between the current position and the future objectives.

(f) *Strategic evaluation and choice.* Evaluating options and deciding which one to follow. This might include financial analysis such as NPV calculations.
(g) *Strategic implementation.* Putting the strategies into practice including polices and strategies for:
- marketing
- finance
- R&D
- IT
- human resources
- quality management
- production.
(h) *Review and control.* Evaluating the success of the strategy by measuring actual performance against objectives and taking control action by amending future strategies and objectives.

Advantages of the rational approach

- long-term approach
- clear purpose and direction
- ongoing learning through review and control
- plans based on detailed analysis
- goal congruence (plans are made which are consistent throughout the organisation).

Disadvantages of planned strategies

- time commitment
- cost (people's time, collecting information, using strategy consultants)
- lack of flexibility (the organisation is constrained by the plan).

Typical usage

- Most common in large organisations.
- Best where there is relatively little change.

The resource-based view of strategy

A resource-based view of strategy suggests that the key to developing a successful strategy is to focus on the firm's unique competences and resources and develop these so they are the best in the market. The firm should then aim to sell products which capitalise on these competences or resources.

Implications for firms include

- A need to ascertain which skills or resources are unique and hard to replicate by others.
- Continued development of these skills/resources.
- Possible outsourcing of other activities so internal focus is on developing the core competences.
- A focus on business processes and how to develop and improve these.

Problems with the resource-based view

- The unique competency is no longer required by customers.
- Competitors find a more successful approach or better way of operating that undermines the competence.

The ecological perspective on the firm – The adaptive or evolutionary approach to strategy

The ecology model suggests that the key to organisational success is to continually adapt and change with the external environment. This ensures that the business remains in a competitive position in relation to competitors and so remains successful. The business therefore "evolves" with its environment to continue to be successful in the same way that organisms have evolved to adapt to their local environments to survive.

This adaptive or positioning-based strategy approach, which pays great attention to markets, consumers and competitors, may be contrasted with the resource-based approach.

Ghoshal and Bartlett suggest that these "Individualised Corporations" have three distinguishing characteristics:

1. They inspire creativity and initiative in their people.
2. They continually learn and develop.
3. They regularly renew themselves (i.e. new processes, products, approaches, etc.).

Problems with the ecological-based view include

- Positioning advantages may be easily copied so the gain is only short term.
- Environmental change may be too rapid to continually adapt the business successfully.
- Continual change means the organisation never truly excels at any one thing.

The emergent strategy approach to strategy formulation (Mintzberg)

Mintzberg's research suggested that real world strategies often arise out of the course of business operations rather than from a formal planning process. Such strategies are called emergent strategies. Directors should be constantly aware of changes in the external environment and bring in new strategies and discard old ones which are not working as the environment changes.

Emergent strategies can be combined with the successful elements of the planned strategy to define the way forward for the business. The process of bringing these together is called *crafting a strategy*. This is more appropriate for businesses in a changing environment, where restriction to one planned strategy may be a competitive weakness.

Logical incrementalism

Logical incrementalism involves the development of strategy using a series of small-scale changes. Plans are not made for the long term as in the rational model, but instead a series of short-term targets and plans are made to continuously move the organisation forward.

Such an approach

- avoids conflict with stakeholders who are unlikely to oppose small changes to plans
- is flexible to small environmental changes
- does not allow for major changes, sometimes necessary for an organisation to maintain its competitiveness in rapidly changing markets. (The rational model is more likely to result in such a "revolutionary" change.)

System-based views on strategy (Mintzberg)

Mintzberg argues that organisational systems pursue their own goals and strategies may therefore be developed due to the "organisational system" rather than what is necessarily for the true benefit of shareholders. Systems goals include

Survival — Employees want to keep their jobs. Directors do not want to be seen to be leading a failed organisation. Organisational survival may therefore be pursued beyond the needs of the shareholders, who in a declining market might be better off if the company was simply liquidated or sold off.

Efficiency — Efficiency is easy to measure through cost savings and productivity improvements. Effectiveness (e.g. customer satisfaction, quality products) is often harder to measure. Organisations are often therefore good at measuring and controlling efficiency but less good at improving effectiveness.

Control — Organisations may aim to control the environment in which they operate by acting to reduce risks. While this may smooth profits or encourage stability for employees it may not be in the best long-term interests of shareholders.

Growth — Directors and managers benefit from organisational growth through bonuses and improved status so will pursue growth even when this is not the best option for the business.

Knowledge test – Quick questions

1.1 Complete the gaps in this definition of business strategy from CIMA official terminology:

"A course of action, including the specification of _____ required, to achieve a specific _____"

1.2 Which of the following is an ADVANTAGE of the rational planning approach to strategy formulation?

- A Goal congruence
- B Time commitment
- C Cost
- D Flexibility

1.3 What are the different three levels of strategy seen in organisations?

- A Corporate, Business and Operational
- B Corporate, Tactical and Emergent
- C Business, Tactical and Emergent
- D Operational, Incremental and Emergent

1.4 Which of the following is not an advantage of the rational approach to strategy formulation?

    A Plans are based on detailed analysis
    B It provides a long-term approach
    C It gives the organisation clear purpose and direction
    D It allows for flexibility

1.5 What might be defined as "A course of action, including the specification of resources required, to achieve a specific objective" (CIMA official terminology)?

    A Strategy
    B Mission
    C Objectives
    D Tactics

1.6 In which stage of the Rational Planning process would a SWOT analysis most likely to be used?

    A Mission
    B Environmental analysis
    C Strategic control
    D Corporate appraisal

1.7 Which of the following is not a distinguishing characteristic of "Individualised Corporations" as suggested by Ghoshal and Bartlett?

    A They inspire creativity and initiative in their people
    B They continually learn and develop
    C They regularly renew themselves
    D They manage stability and patterns

1.8 There are a number of ways of forming strategy. Which one of the following is such a method?

    A Incrementalism
    B Integrationalism
    C Internationalism
    D Internalism

1.9 Mintzberg identified four system goals. Which of the following is not one of them?

    A Survival
    B Profit maximisation
    C Efficiency
    D Growth

1.10 An organisation which uses its past strategy as a guide to the future strategy? This is best described by what method of strategy formation?

    A Incrementalism
    B Freewheeling opportunism
    C Rational planning
    D Crafting

1.11 What is the process of bringing together emergent strategies with the successful elements of the planned strategy to define the way forward for the business known as?

   A   Crafting
   B   Incrementalism
   C   Implementation
   D   Resource based

1.12 "The resources of the decision maker are limited and decision making is the result of the trade off between the quality of the decision and the cost of reaching it, in terms of time and information gathering and processing". What is the name given to this model of decision-making?

   A   Emergent strategy
   B   Rational planning
   C   Logical incrementalism
   D   Bounded rationality

Knowledge test – Answers

1.1 "A course of action, including the specification of resources required, to achieve a specific objective"

1.2 **A**

   Plans are made which are consistent throughout the organisation.

1.3 **A**

   The three different levels of strategy are

   1. *Corporate strategy* – set by the board or other senior management
   2. *Business strategy* – set by divisional management at business unit level
   3. *Functional strategies* – co-ordinates and improves activities of the business unit.

1.4 **D**

   One of the disadvantages of the rational planning model is the lack of flexibility. Others are the cost and time commitment.

1.5 **A**

   This is the official CIMA terminology for Business Strategy.

1.6 **D**

   Corporate appraisal is a summary of the current position of the organisation, often using a SWOT analysis which summarises the organisation's strengths, weaknesses, opportunities and threats.

1.7 **D**

   Managing stability and patterns is one of the essential activities in strategic management according to Mintzberg.

1.8 **A**

Logical incrementalism was identified by Quinn. It describes taking small, seemingly insignificant steps towards a goal.

1.9 **B**

The missing system goal is control. Organisations may aim to control the environment in which they operate by acting to reduce risks. While this may smooth profits or encourage stability for employees it may not be in the best long-term interests of shareholders.

1.10 **A**

1.11 **A**

This is appropriate for businesses in a changing environment, where restriction to one planned strategy may be a competitive weakness.

1.12 **D**

Simon argued that the decision-making of people is limited and is bound by time, information and other factors when making decisions.

Assessing the External Environment

Assessing the External Environment

2

✎ Examining the broader environment – PEST analysis

PEST analysis provides four key factors against which to review how the broad environment will effect the business. Strategies can then be developed which address any potential opportunities and threats identified.

Political/legal

Things to consider include

- government spending
- policies of new governments
- new legislation
- tax changes
- tariffs and trade barriers – foreign trade
- foreign laws when operating in different countries
- employment law
- regulation (e.g. telecoms).

Economic

Things to consider include

- interest rates
- exchange rates
- current strength of economy
- inflation rates
- overseas economies.

Social

Things to consider include

- Demographic changes
  - population movements
  - ageing population.

- Social trends
  - greater use of IT and mobile communications
  - internet usage
  - health and fitness
  - changing working styles (e.g. remote working)
  - increase in litigation.

Technical

Things to consider include

- new purchasing mechanisms (intranet, extranet)
- new production technology
- new distribution mechanisms (internet)
- new methods of working (e.g. mobile telecommunications)
- opportunities for new products to sell.

Examining industry profitability – Porter's five forces

Porter's five forces model is used to examine the profitability of an industry, and is a useful tool to clarify whether to enter or exit the market. Competing firms can also act to change the forces to make the market more profitable for them.

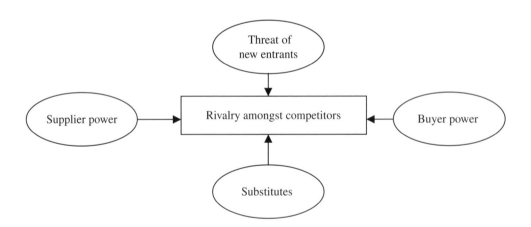

Competitors

Key factors which create a high force are

- lots of competitors
- similar products (so firms compete on price)
- strong competitors
- declining market size
- exit barriers (e.g. high cost of leaving a market). This keeps competitors in a market they might otherwise leave.

Threat of new entrants

This is the threat that new competitors will enter the market driving prices down.

The threat of new entrants will be low when there are significant *barriers to entry*. These can include

- high costs to set up the business
- legal barriers (e.g. licences, patents)
- cost advantages of existing competitors are significant (e.g. due to scale of operation)
- significant competition in the industry
- existing competitors have strong brands.

Buyer power

This is the power of customers over the competitors in the industry.

Key factors which create a high force are

- few customers
- large customers who provide a large proportion of company profits
- customers can easily and readily switch between competitors.

Supplier power

This is the power of suppliers over people in the industry.

Key factors which create a high force are

- few alternative suppliers
- cost of changing suppliers is high.

Substitute products

Substitutes are products which fulfil the same needs as the needs met by the product in the industry being examined. A substitute of trains might be coaches, buses or cars for example.

If customers can have their needs met from many different types of products they will react to increases in prices or poorer service by switching to substitute products. This makes profitability in the industry low.

Porter's Diamond – The competitive of a nation's industries

Michael Porter's "The Competitive Advantage of Nations" suggested that some nations' industries succeed more than others in terms of international competition. This will lead to a cluster of successful firms in a country.

Competitor advantage can be explained by the presence of four determinants. Each element is capable of enhancing national competitive advantage. These are outlined in the diagram below:

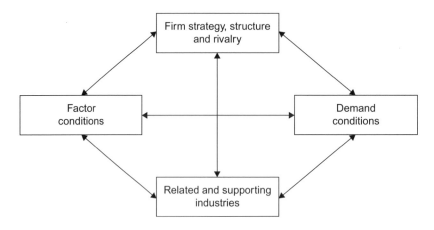

Factor conditions

Factor conditions are the resources that a country has. These Porter splits into

- *Basic factors:* These factors require little or no investment; natural resources, climate, semiskilled and unskilled labour.
- *Advanced factors:* These factors have needed investment in the past; communications infrastructure and skilled labour.

Demand conditions

Demanding consumers in the domestic market puts pressure on firms to innovate.

Related and supporting industries

Competitive success in one industry is linked to success in related industries.

Firm strategy, structure and rivalry

Strong domestic rivalry is important because it increases the pressure to innovate.

Interactions between the determinants

The factors in the Diamond are interrelated. Competitor advantage rarely rests on only one element of the Diamond.

Knowledge test – Quick questions

2.1 When examining the external environment, organisations might use PEST analysis. What does PEST stand for?

    A Political, Environmental, Social and Technical
    B Physical, Environmental, Social and Technical

C   Physical, Emergent, Strategic and Turbulent
   D   Political, Economic, Social and Technical

2.2 Which of the following could NOT be a use of Porter's five forces model?

   A   To explain the levels of profitability in an industry.
   B   To explain the concentration of world leading organisations in some countries.
   C   To guide an organisation on how it may improve its own profitability.
   D   To analyse the attractiveness of a market for a new entrant.

2.3 Using Porter's five forces model to examine the profitability of an industry which of the following, everything else being equal, will lead to higher profitability?

   A   An increase in buyer power
   B   A new entrant into the industry
   C   A new supplier to the industry
   D   The development of an alternative product meeting the needs of the industries' customers

2.4 A country's superior road network would be classified as what in Porter's Diamond?

   A   A basic factor
   B   An advanced factor
   C   Related and supporting industry
   D   Supplier power

Knowledge test – Answers

2.1 **D**

PEST analysis provides four key factors against which to review how the broad environment will effect the business. Strategies can then be developed which address any potential opportunities and threats identified.

2.2 **B**

This solution describes another of Porter's models – The comparative advantage of nations model.

2.3 **C**

A new supplier to the industry will lead to lower costs as that industry will become more competitive. This in turn will, everything else being equal, increase the profitability for the industry which it is supplying.

2.4 **B**

An advanced factor. Advanced factors have needed investment in the past e.g communications infrastructure, skilled labour or a road infrastructure.

Strategic Models and Tools

Strategic Models and Tools 3

Mission

An organisation's mission outlines the reasons for existence of the organisation, what it is aiming to achieve and why. A mission helps to

- provide a common sense of identity and purpose for employees
- direct strategic decision-making
- set relevant objectives
- communicate the organisation's purpose to stakeholders.

A mission statement outlines the company's mission. Qualities of good mission statements are

- clear/unambiguous
- concise
- covers the whole organisation
- open ended (not quantifiable).

Contents of good mission statements (per Campbell et al.):

(a) *Purpose*

- For whom does it exist?
- What does the organisation do for these people?
- What does the organisation hope to achieve in the long term?

(b) *Strategy*

- How will the organisation compete?
- The range of businesses it is operating within.

(c) *Values*

- Principles which the organisation will uphold (quality, value for money, innovation, etc.).

(d) *Policies*

- Policies people must follow which ensure they act according to the defined values, strategy and purpose.

Objectives

A mission is non-quantifiable, that is, it provides an overall direction and purpose rather than being directly measurable. This means it is very hard to measure its success and it is not a good tool for motivating staff since targets are unclear.

For a mission to be effective, it needs to be supported by clear, measurable objectives which provide targets for directors and staff, and hence motivates and provides focus for them.

They also perform an important role in performance measurement as organisational and individual performance can be assessed by how effectively objectives have been achieved.

Hierarchy of objectives

Objectives are set at different levels within the organisation to motivate and focus performance in each major part of the business. This goes right down to the individuals who are set objectives as part of their appraisal.

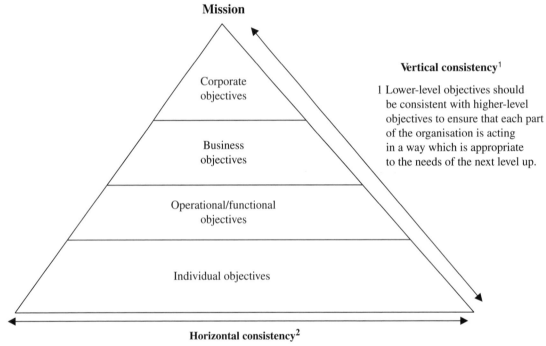

SMART objectives

To be effective, objectives should have the following qualities:

(a) **S**pecific
(b) **M**easurable
(c) **A**chievable
(d) **R**elevant (related to the mission or area of responsibility of the individual/division)
(e) **T**ime bound.

Stakeholders

Stakeholders of an organisation are people who are interested in or effected in some way by the operation of the organisation.

Organisational objectives should always be considered in relation to the objectives of different stakeholders. This ensures that a wide range of needs are considered in the objective-setting process and balanced objectives are produced.

Johnson and Scholes put stakeholders into three key categories. Each stakeholders has different interests and needs in relation to the organisation.

Category	Stakeholder	Needs/requirements
Internal	Directors	Pay, bonus, overall company performance, job security
	Employees	Pay, bonus, personal performance, job security
Connected	Shareholders	Share price growth, dividend payments
	Customers	Prices, quality, delivery times, assured supply
	Suppliers	Assured custom, high prices
	Financiers	Interest payments, ability to pay back loans
External	Government	Tax, law, well-being of nation's people (e.g. health) e.g.
	Pressure groups	Environmental issues
	Local community	Employment, nice place to live
	Wider community	Environment

From an accountant's perspective, key stakeholders include:

- *Tax professionals* – providing corporate and personal tax advice, including completion of tax returns.
- *External auditors* – who review the financial statements to check their truth and fairness.
- *Legal advisers*.
- *Investors and financiers* – who want regular updates on the company's position and strategies so they can ensure their investment is secure and support investment decisions. They also receive full audited financial statements annually to ensure they understand the true financial position of the company.

Mendelow's power/interest matrix

Mendelow's matrix helps to identify the relationships that should be built with different stakeholders. A stakeholder's position in the matrix depends on two factors:

(i) The power to influence the organisation, and effect its decision-making.

   A large customer may have significant power and the organisation will change products, prices, location of production facilities and so on to meet this customers needs. Small customers have far less power and their needs are unlikely to be prioritised.

(ii) The interest which the stakeholder has in the organisation.

   The greater the interest in the organisation the greater the level of communication that will be required with them. Many employees have little power, but good communication of plans is important to retain their loyalty and motivation.

	Low	Interest	High
Low		Minimal interest (e.g. Temporary employee)	Keep informed (e.g. Office worker)
Power			
High		Keep satisfied (e.g. Government)	Key player – keep close (e.g. Family shareholder)

Corporate appraisal – SWOT analysis

A corporate appraisal is an overview of the organisation's current position and summarises the internal and external position of the firm.

As the company works towards achieving its objectives, the corporate appraisal is a summary of the company's

(a) strengths
(b) weaknesses
(c) opportunities
(d) threats.

The company must develop a strategy which

(a) capitalises on and continues to build the strengths
(b) overcomes or mitigates the impact of weaknesses
(c) takes suitable opportunities
(d) overcomes or mitigates the threats.

The level of decision-making

Centralisation

Centralisation is where the majority of decisions are made by senior management or by a centralised function (e.g. the group marketing function defining marketing approaches to be followed by all divisions). Few decisions are delegated to lower level managers who simply carry out the orders of senior management or centralised function.

Advantages

1. Goal congruence (decisions should be best for the organisation as a whole).
2. Duplication of tasks/decision-making is reduced.
3. Reduced costs through economies of scale (e.g. purchasing in bulk for the whole organisation).
4. Standardised processes ensure consistency of approach throughout the organisation.

Decentralisation

In a decentralised organisation authority is delegated down the structure to divisional or lower level managers who make their own decisions.

Advantages

1. Decisions are made by staff with a clear understanding of departmental issues (e.g. the US division makes decisions based on their knowledge of the US market rather than those being made by a manager at head office in the UK).
2. Motivating for lower level managers.
3. Decision-making is quick and efficient.
4. Enables staff to gain managerial experience.
5. Senior management are free to concentrate on strategic issues.

Organisations can use a mixture of both a centralised and decentralised approach for different decisions. For example, the global brand might be developed at head office, but the specific marketing approach used might be allowed to vary country by country depending on local markets.

The value chain

The value chain outlines the key activities which are undertaken by an organisation. Each of these activities aims to *add value* to the input costs so that the end products or services can be sold for a profit (creating a profit margin). By examining its activities and ensuring that they all support each other, the organisation can

- remove non-value-adding activities (those which add little to the end customer but which are incurring costs)
- add more value to customers.

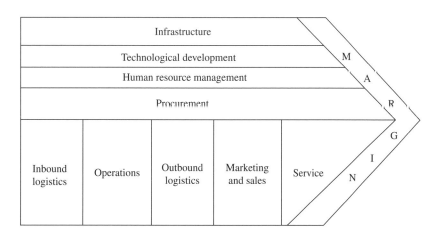

The key activities outlined by Porter were broken down into Primary and Support activities.

Primary activities

- *Inbound logistics.* All activities required to receive, store and distribute inputs such as raw materials.
- *Operations.* The main business of the firm, which convert inputs into products and services. In a manufacturing organisation this would be production; in a retail organisation, managing and running retail outlets.
- *Outbound logistics.* Activities required to collect, store and distribute the output.
- *Marketing and sales.* Activities which inform buyers about products and services, induce buyers to purchase them and facilitate their purchase.
- *Service.* After sales-service including warranties, servicing and product support.

Support activities

- *Procurement.* The acquisition of raw materials, services, fixed assets, including the management of suppliers.
- *Human resource management.* Including training, recruitment, redundancy, appraisal, scheduling, pay and any other people-related activity.
- *Technological development.* Computer hardware and software and new operating procedures.
- *Infrastructure.* Consists of other support functions or departments such as accounting, legal, finance, planning, public affairs, government relations, quality assurance and general management.

The finance function's role in adding value

The finance function has a specific role in relation to adding value through the measurement of the costs of individual processes, and business operations, to identify the activities which are truly adding value to the organisation and those which are not.

Specific issues for the finance function over recent years include

- *Business process outsourcing* – where external organisations take over previously internal processes (e.g. IT or manufacturing). Benefits include

    - Greater expertise of experienced external companies
    - Potentially lower costs, as they may have economies of scale
    - Clear standards as set down in the service contract, which should ensure quality.

    Accountants may be involved in weighing up the benefits and drawbacks of outsourcing versus providing the service in-house. The process of comparing costs of all elements of outsourcing (including often missed costs like legal costs, ongoing contract management and dispute resolution) is called *transaction cost theory*.

- *Shared service centres* – where common tasks are undertaken centrally rather than in a local divisions. Commonly shared service centres include mostly administrative tasks or specific functions like IT which are common to everyone. They can provide consistency and reduce costs.
- Making finance personal part of strategic and business decision processes – this ensures that all decisions take into account two key elements:

    - Cost/benefit analysis e.g. using NPV, IRR and other related techniques
    - Financing the investment e.g. sourcing the money, cashflow implications.

Porter's generic strategies

Firms that are more profitable than the average in the industry have a competitive advantage over the other companies in the industry. Michael Porter said that to be competitive every organisation must be either a cost leader or have a differentiated product or service.

Cost leadership

The cost leader is the lowest cost producer in the market. This enables the cost leader to sell at a lower price than competitors and remain profitable, giving it a competitive advantage.

Cost leadership can be achieved by minimising costs throughout the value chain. For example, through

- efficient production/purchasing processes
- using low-cost materials
- reducing support costs
- designing products for low-cost manufacturing
- generating economies of scale through mass production.

Differentiation

A differentiated product or service offers unique features that are valued by customers' and that customers perceive to be better than or different from competitors' products or services.

The value added by the uniqueness of the product allows the firm to charge a premium price enabling it to be profitable and compete in the same market as cost leaders.

Differentiation can be achieved through

- product features (e.g. style, add-ons)
- high-quality products
- good customer service
- branding image.

Focus

Both cost leadership and differentiation policies can be followed with either a broad focus (selling to all customers in the market) or narrow focus (selling to specific segments of the market). Operating with a narrow focus enables firms to specialise without having to invest large sums to meet all customer needs.

The organisation can follow one of four "generic strategies".

	Low cost	Differentiated
Broad (FOCUS)	Cost leadership	Differentiation
Narrow (FOCUS)	Cost focus	Differentiation focus

Being "stuck in the middle"

Firms which do not have a clear generic strategy are "stuck in the middle" and according to Michael Porter are unlikely to be successful in the long term due to their weak competitive position.

Knowledge test – Quick questions

3.1 What are the contents of an effective mission statement according to Campbell?

  A Purpose, Strategy, Values, Policies
  B Open ended, Concise, Inclusive, Clear
  C Purpose, Strategy, Values, Principles
  D Principles, Strategy, Clarity, Values

3.2 Objectives are quantified measures of Mission. Which of the following is NOT a quality they should possess?

  A Time bound
  B Centralised
  C Achievable
  D Specific

3.3 What sort of stakeholders might shareholders be described as (using Johnson and Scholes model)?

  A Internal
  B Key players
  C Connected
  D External

3.4 In which classification would a stakeholder who has *low interest* and *high power* be (using Mendelow's matrix)?

  A Minimal interest
  B Keep informed
  C Keep satisfied
  D Key player

3.5 Which of the following is an advantage of the entrepreneurial/simple structure.

  A Highly adaptable to changing business circumstances.
  B Lack of control as the organisation grows since the MD becomes unable to control everything.
  C There may be a lack of specialists, compared with a functional organisation.
  D The MD/owner does not maintain control of operations.

3.6 Which of the following in NOT an advantage of the Functional structure to organisational design?

  A Specialists expertise in each business function ensures tasks are done to a high quality.
  B Each major business task is managed and controlled.
  C Clear responsibilities enable clearly measurable department objectives, which helps to motivate managers to ensure their department is successful.
  D Lack of interdepartmental communication.

3.7 What is the term to describe the situation where the majority of decisions are made by senior management? Few decisions are delegated to lower level managers who simply carry out the orders of senior management.

  A Centralisation
  B Decentralisation
  C Differentiation
  D Bureaucracy

3.8 Objectives are set at different levels within the organisation to motivate and focus performance. Once the mission of the organisation has been decided upon, the objectives may then be decided. Starting at the top of the hierarchy of objectives, what is the order in which these objectives should be set?

  A Individual, Operational, Business, Corporate
  B Corporate, Business, Operational, Individual
  C Corporate, Operational, Business, Individual
  D Individual, Business, Operational, Corporate

3.9 Using Johnson and Scholes categories, which of the following are connected stakeholders:

- Directors
- Shareholders
- Suppliers
- Government
- Local community
- Employees
- Customers
- Financiers
- Pressure groups
- Wider community

3.10 Cost leadership may be achieved by ALL of the following except which one

  A Efficiency improvements
  B Economy in purchasing
  C Effectiveness in output
  D Economies of scale

3.11 Which of the following is NOT a support activity?

  A Marketing and sales
  B Procurement
  C Technological development

✓ Knowledge test – Answers

3.1 **A**

Contents of good mission statements (per Campbell et al.):

(a) *Purpose*

- For whom does it exist?
- What does the organisation do for these people?
- What does the organisation hope to achieve in the long term?

(b) *Strategy*

- How will the organisation compete?
- The range of businesses it is operating within.

(c) *Values*

- Principles which the organisation will uphold (quality, value for money, innovation, etc.).

(d) *Policies*

- Policies people must follow which ensure they act according to the defined values, strategy and purpose.

3.2 **B**

To be effective, objectives should have the following qualities:

(a) **S**pecific
(b) **M**easurable
(c) **A**chievable
(d) **R**elevant (related to the mission or area of responsibility of the individual/division)
(e) **T**ime bound.

3.3 **C**

3.4. **C**

Mendelow's matrix helps to identify the relationships that should be built with different stakeholders.

3.5 **A**

The advantages of the *entrepreneurial/simple structure* are

- Highly adaptable to changing business circumstances. Unlike other structures there is littlew formality in the structure and therefore little bureaucracy.
- The MD/owner maintains control of operations.
- Useful for small organisations where the MD can effectively manage all employees.

3.6 **D**

This is a disadvantage of the functional structure. The other disadvantages are inter-departmental conflict, lack of goal congruence (people act for the benefit of their department not the organisation as a whole) and the organisation may become bureaucratic as rules and procedures are used to control work.

3.7 **A**

3.8 **B**

Objectives should start at the top of the organisation with the corporate strategy. Care should be taken to ensure that there is both vertical and horizontal consistency.

3.9
- Shareholders
- Customers
- Suppliers
- Financiers.

3.10 **C**

Effectiveness in output is the ability of the product to meet the needs of the consumer and may not lead to lower costs – in fact perhaps the opposite.

3.11 **A**

Marketing and sales are activities which inform buyers and sellers about products and services, induce buyers to purchase them and facilitate their purchase.

Organisational Culture, Ethics and Governance

Organisational Culture, Ethics and Governance   4

Culture

Culture is a combination of the organisation's

- Values
- Attitudes
- Norms
- Expectations.

Individuals often act within the standard norms of group behaviour. If, for example, people generally take a short lunch break it is likely that a new employee will too, even if this is not stated in the company's policies. Such cultural norms can have a dramatic effect on the organisation and success, particularly when such norms relate to attitudes to

- working hard or long hours
- loyalty
- innovation
- quality
- customers
- meeting deadlines
- support for others.

Influences on culture

The culture of an organisation can be influenced by many factors including

- directors
- owners
- staff
- firm history
- national cultures
- organisational structure
- strategic approach.

Importance of culture

Culture is important since it

- influences behaviours

    Cultural issues might therefore need to be addressed as part of
    - change management programmes
    - ethical programmes
    - quality management
    - HR programmes (e.g. to improve staff motivation or efficiency).

- ensures consistency of approach even where no set rules exist
- can cause conflict
    - between different groups internally who have different cultures
    - between customers and suppliers
    - between organisation's who merge or are acquired.

Cultural control

Control over culture can be exercised through

- statement of values outlining what the organisation stands for
- training
- recruitment of staff with new beliefs, values or approaches
- senior management being seen to act in a new way
- new rules and procedures – clarifying expected behaviours
- new symbols (e.g. buildings, job titles, logos)
- changing groups and structures
- new reward systems encouraging new behaviour.

Cultural models

Handy

Handy generalised organisations into four overriding types of culture:

1. Power culture

    - one central source of power, typically an owner/managing director
    - few procedures or rules
    - quick to react and change.

    Often found in small organisations.

2. Role culture

    - formal rules and procedures
    - formal structure with clear responsibilities for each individual
    - people act in accordance with rules and requirements of their position.

    This bureaucratic approach is often found in large public organisations or functionally structured organisations.

3. Task culture

- focus on getting the job done, be that: providing customer service, developing new products, changing processes, and so on
- people focus on their current task rather than their role
- good communication.

Often associated with matrix structures, for example, consultancy firm.

4. Person culture

- organisation exists to satisfy the requirements of the individual
- individuals operate independently.

For example, Barristers' Chambers.

Ethics and social responsibility

Ethics are a code of moral principles that people follow with respect to what is right or wrong.

Examples might include

- legal conformance
- paying a generous redundancy package
- safety at work.

Social responsibility is the duty the organisation has towards the wider community or society.

Examples might include

- supporting charity
- environmental issues
- public safety
- exploitation of third-world workers.

Why are they important?

Ethical issues can have a number of advantages:

- generate good feeling amongst staff
- avoid legal action
- avoid bad publicity and the potential damage to reputation which might result
- as a source of competitive advantage.

Ethical control

There are three key ways to control ethics within an organisation:

(i) Personal ethics

These are the moral principles held by individuals.

The ethics of the organisation will closely reflect the ethics of its staff. This is particularly true of the senior management in an organisation since they make the significant decisions. They are also role models for other staff and so their behaviour may influence that of other staff.

Control over personal ethics can be exercised through employing people with suitable ethical principles. This might be through making it a part of the recruitment procedure through references being taken or checks on personal histories.

(ii) Organisational culture

The culture is the combination of the beliefs, values and standards of behaviour inherent in an organisation. Often behaviours are influenced by what is seen to be right or wrong within the group of employees. A group "ethical stance" may well develop which is adhered to by its members and perpetuated through others learning what is acceptable within the group.

Control can be exercised through

- Statement of values outlining what the organisation stands for. Values such as integrity, fairness, truthfulness might encourage ethical approach to work.
- Communication of ethical expectations (e.g. on induction programmes).
- Senior management leading the way by behaving ethically themselves and supporting ethical behaviour in others.

(iii) Organisational systems

These are the sets of internal processes and activities which dictate the way the organisation operates. The development of organisational systems around ethical issues can facilitate ethical control. These could include

- reward systems – to reward good ethical behaviour
- recruitment systems – to recruit the right people
- ethical codes outlining strict behavioural rules to be followed
- ethical audits – a review of a department's ethical behaviour
- disciplinary procedures to be used when people break ethical rules.

CIMA code of ethics

A member of a profession, such as an accountant, will be expected to apply the set of ethical principles adopted by their professional body as standards of professional behaviour that its members are expected to adhere to. CIMA's ethical principles have been adopted based on those suggested by the International Federation of Accountants (IFAC), and they are:

Integrity means being straightforward, honest and truthful in all professional and business relationships. People should not be associated with any information that they believe contains a materially false or misleading statement, or which is misleading because it omits or obscures the facts.

Objectivity means not allowing bias, conflict of interest or the influence of other people to override professional judgement. To protect your objectivity, you should avoid relationships that could bias or overly influence your professional opinion.

Professional competence and due care is an ongoing commitment to maintain a level of professional knowledge and skill. Each individual should ensure that their employer or customer/client should receive a competent and professional service. Updates should be undertaken on current developments in the individual's area of work, legislation and regulation.

Confidentiality means respecting the confidential nature of information acquired through professional relationships such as past or current employment. Information should not be disclosed unless the individual has specific permission or a legal or professional duty to do so. Confidential information should never be used for the individual's or or another person's advantage.

Professional behaviour requires individuals to comply with relevant laws and regulations. Professionals, such as accountants, must also avoid any action that could negatively affect the reputation of their profession.

Corporate governance

The directors run the organisation on behalf of shareholders. The needs of the directors and shareholders may not always be consistent however, which may result in the directors making decisions which are not in the best interests of employees. Codes of corporate governance ensure that the directors run the company in the best interests of the owners.

During the 1990s a number of approaches to corporate governance were outlined in the Cadbury code and the Greenbury and Hampel reports. The findings of these reports were brought together in the combined code which requires the directors of listed companies to report under by the stock exchange. Some of the key elements of the combined code include

- Separation of the roles of chairman and chief executive so no one person has too much control at the top of the organisation.
- The board should contain both executive directors (who undertake the day-to-day running of the business) and non-executive directors (who act as independent advisers and have a role to ensure shareholder's best interests are met).
- Executive director's employment contracts should not exceed three years. This ensures shareholders can remove a director without having to pay very long-term contracts. Note that this does not prevent contracts being renewed.
- Remuneration should be sufficient but not excessive.
- Full and clear disclosure of directors' emoluments should be made.
- Executive director pay should be determined by a remuneration committee made up of non-executive directors.

Note that the combined code is not compulsory. Disclosure only needs to be made as to whether these principles have been upheld.

Encouraging innovation and creativity

Internal innovation and creativity are vital to the success of most modern organisations. This is because of the following:

- Changing customer demands
- Increasingly competitive markets
- Technological innovations
- Globalisation

- Overseas competition
- Opportunities for cheaper operations
- New markets to exploit.

Organisations which are not flexible to the markets around them are likely to fail in the long term.

Benefits

- Meet customer needs
- New products produced, giving increased revenue and profits
- New markets reached, again generating additional profits
- Overcome threats from competitors
- Creates a dynamic, exciting culture for staff to work in.

Drawbacks

- Many innovations fail, which may demoralise staff
- Costly to undertake – research, development and implementation
- Change is required, which often results in staff resistance.

Knowledge test – Quick questions

4.1 A culture where there is one central source of power and few procedures or rules would be classified by Handy as what sort of culture?

 A Power
 B Role
 C Task
 D Person

4.2 A culture where organisation exists to satisfy the requirements of the individual and individuals operate independently would be classified by Handy as what sort of culture?

 A Power
 B Role
 C Task
 D Person

4.3 During the 1990s a number of approaches to corporate governance were outlined in the Cadbury code and the Greenbury and Hampel reports. Which of the following were NOT key elements of the combined report:

 A Separation of the roles of chairman and chief executive so no one person has too much control at the top of the organisation.
 B The board should contain both executive directors (who undertake the day-to-day running of the business) and non-executive directors (who act as independent advisers and have a role to ensure shareholder's best interests are met).
 C Executive director's employment contracts should not exceed three years. This ensures shareholders can remove a director without having to pay very long-term contracts. Note that this does not prevent contracts being renewed.

D   Executive director pay should be determined by a remuneration committee made up of executive directors.

4.4 Using Handy's classifications of culture, how would you describe the likely culture found in both Barristers' Chambers and hippy commune?

A   Power
B   Role
C   Task
D   Person

4.5 Using Handy's classifications of culture how would you describe the culture most likely to be found in the civil service?

A   Power
B   Role
C   Task
D   Person

4.6 Aracnia Training is a small entrepreneurial organisation led by Darryl Cain, who started up the business 4 years ago. Darryl is central to all the key decisions made in the firm, which now has 22 employees. His knowledge and business awareness is very important to the firm's success. According to Handy's cultural model, which type of culture does Aracnia have?

A   Power
B   Role
C   Task
D   Person

4.7 BNJ Frome is a networking group of many owners and managers of small- and medium-sized businesses in the Frome area. Members meet for breakfast each week and exchange contacts for the mutual benefit of other members. According to Handy's cultural model, which of type of culture does BNJ Frome have?

A   Power
B   Role
C   Task
D   Person

4.8 Non-executive directors can perform an important role in corporate governance in all but one of the following ways:

A   They act as independent advisers ensuring that executive directors make decisions in the best interest of shareholders.
B   They are responsible for all key business decisions so they should ensure that shareholders interests are taken into account.
C   They lay a role on the renumeration committee to ensure fair pay to directors.
D   They are members of the audit committee to whom internal and external auditors report.

4.9 Briefly explain the difference between ethics and social responsibility.

(2 marks)

Knowledge test – Answers

4.1 **A**

Power culture is characterised by one central source of power, typically an owner/managing director, few procedures or rules and quick to react and change.

4.2 **B**

An example of this might be Barristers' Chambers.

4.3 **D**

The executive directors pay should be determined by a remuneration committee made up of NON-executive directors.

4.4 **D**

Using Handy's classification, the Person classifications of culture is how you would describe the likely culture found in both Barristers' Chambers and hippy commune.

4.5 **B**

Using Handy's classification the role classifications of culture is how you would describe the likely culture found in the civil service. The culture would be manifested in:
- formal rules and procedures
- formal structure with clear responsibilities for each individual
- people act in accordance with rules and requirements of their position.

4.6 **A**

Aracnia Training is likely to have a power culture, which is characterised by an organisation which has one central source of power, typically an owner/managing director, few procedures or rules and is quick to react and change. A role culture has many formal rules and procedures with a clear role focus for individuals. A task culture focuses on getting the job done, and there is good communication and commonly a project or customer focus. In a person culture, the organisation exists to satisfy the requirements of the individual. Although people operate independently they benefit from being part of a group.

4.7 **D**

BNJ Frome has a person culture. In a person culture, the organisation exists to satisfy the requirements of the individual. Although people operate independently they benefit from being part of a group. A power culture is characterised by an organisation which has one central source of power, typically an owner/managing director, few procedures or rules and is quick to react and change. A role culture has many formal rules and procedures with a clear role focus for individuals. A task culture focuses on getting the job done, and there is good communication and commonly a project or customer focus.

4.8 **B**

The executive directors are responsible for most decision-making not the non-executives.

4.9 Ethics are a code of moral principles that people follow with respect to what is right or wrong. Whereas social responsibility is the duty of the organisation towards the wider community or society.

Introduction to Project Management

Introduction to Project Management   5

Projects and project management

Projects

 The Association of Project Managers defines a project as

"A human activity that achieves a clear objective against a timescale."

The term "project" is often used to describe something outside of normal day-to-day repetitive work. It is often characterised by

- a one-off event
- clear objective
- set timescale
- project manager organising and controlling the project
- project team charged with executing the project
- resources and budgets allocated
- an end-customer.

In some organisations, such as consultants or builders, the majority of their work is project based.

Project management

"The integration of all aspects of a project, ensuring that the proper knowledge and resources are available when and where needed, and above all to ensure that the expected outcome is proceeded in a timely, cost-effective manner" (CIMA: Official Terminology).

There are nine key areas of project management (as outlined by the Project Management Institute).

Nine key areas	Constituents
Integration	Developing plans Executing plans Controlling change
Scope Time	Defining, planning and controlling the scope Setting objectives
Cost	Defining activities and their duration Sequencing activities Developing time schedules
Quality	Budgeting Cost monitoring Cost control
Resources	Developing a quality plan Quality assurance and control Acquisition and effective management of • staff • materials • buildings • equipment
Communication	Communicating to all stakeholders, including progress reporting
Risk	Identifying and quantifying risk Risk reduction and management
Procurement	Selecting suppliers Negotiating Contracting Monitoring supplier performance

Objectives of project management

The objectives of project management flow directly from these project management areas. They are to ensure

(a) All key parties agree with project objectives.
(b) Risks of failure are considered and minimised.
(c) Costs are monitored and controlled.
(d) The project takes place in the best way through clear planning.
(e) Resources are acquired and used efficiently.
(f) The required standards of quality are met.
(g) All stakeholders are engaged and their needs are met.
(h) To complete the project on time.

Contrast with line management

Line management is the management of day-to-day operations, for example a supervisor managing a production line or a sales manager managing their sales team. Line managers have the same area of responsibility day in day out and manage the same team doing the same basic tasks.

Programme management

Programme Management relates to the management of a portfolio of projects often, but not always, leading to organisational change. It is an overarching function, in which overall goals for the programme are clarified and the projects which will drive that change decided upon. These are then prioritised, planned and coordinated to ensure that not only do the individual projects achieve their objectives but that the combination of projects achieve the change required for the organisation/programme as a whole. As an example, the Olympics will contain a wide range of individual projects in the overall programme. These projects will include construction of a range of venues, IT systems, staff training, planning each event and so on. These all come together into the overall programme designed to produce a successful Olympics for the competitors and spectators.

Stakeholders

Project stakeholders

A stakeholder is anyone who is interested in, is influenced by, or involved in some way with the project.

Project stakeholders include

Project sponsor	Provide overall resources and make the investment decision.
Project board/ project owner	An individual or group of people tasked with overseeing the project. The project manger will periodically report to the project board/owner who will assess progress and have authority delegated to them by the project sponsor to allow significant project changes.
Champion	A champion is usually a senior member of staff who supports the project and will "oil the political wheels" to facilitate its progress.
Customers/client	The end-user, who will ultimately benefit from the project's completion.
Suppliers	Provide materials, assets and services.
Project manager	Responsible for the project and its success.
Project team	Undertake project activities.

In large projects you will usually find people or groups in all these roles. In smaller projects some of these roles may not exist or are undertaken by the same person/group.

Stakeholder communication is vital to successful project management since it achieves buy-in and avoids misunderstandings which can cost time.

Project managers

The role of project management is usually undertaken by a project manager. It is the project manager's responsibility to look after the nine key areas of project management and ensure the project is completed on time, within budget and to the required standard of quality.

To do this they need a variety of skills and knowledge:

Nine key areas	Project manager skills/knowledge
Integration	Change management skills: – Overcoming resistance to change – Change management tools and techniques (e.g. Lewin)
Scope	Project area knowledge (e.g. IT project needs someone with some good understanding of IT)
Time	Use of time-planning models and software
Cost	Costing and budgeting knowledge
Quality	Planning and monitoring
Resources	Leadership skills: – Obtaining results through personal direction and influence – Team participation and consultation – Encouraging team spirit and support – Recognising staff achievement – Conflict resolution Delegation skills: – Communicating overall and individual objectives – Passing down responsibility for tasks – Encouraging individual learning
Communication	Communication skills: – Verbal/people – Report writing – Running meetings
Risk	Problem-solving skills: – Analysing problems – Brainstorming solutions – Decision-making
Procurement	Negotiation skills: – Understanding leverage points – Seeing the buyers perspective – Being willing to walk away

The project team

The project team is responsible for undertaking project activities. To be successful the project team must

- work as a team
- have a good team spirit
- be well co-ordinated and controlled
- be motivated
- have the right skill mix
- have the right mix of personalities (e.g. Belbin)
- be effectively managed through the stages in group development (Tuckman)
- be given clear objectives
- have the appropriate resources
- have clear roles and responsibilities defined to each team member.

Successful group and team working are discussed in more detail in Chapter 10.

Project team structure

The project team must have a clear internal structure. It should have clear leadership (usually from the project manager), and delegated responsibilities to team members for specific parts of the project. The larger the team the larger the team hierarchy is likely to be.

Organisational structure and the link to project success

Organisational structures are discussed earlier in detail in Chapter 3. The likelihood of success of a project may depend on the organisational structure.

Matrix organisations have a structure and internal systems which naturally allow for new projects to start up. Consequences of projects in matrix organisations include

- Project members are likely to be team players since this will be considered as part of the selection process.
- The project management process will be familiar to everyone.
- Obtaining resources will be a straightforward process built into everyday operating procedures.
- Project members will also have responsibility to their department as well as the project, and may have to spend time on departmental duties (e.g. departmental meetings) while on the project.

In divisional or functional organisations, where project working is less common, the culture may be more resistant to project-based working and project members less experienced at working in project teams and in a project environment.

Knowledge test – Quick questions

5.1 Who is responsible for overseeing the progress of a project and authorising major project changes?

    A Project champion
    B Project manager
    C Project sponsor
    D Project board

5.2 In which of the following organisational structures are projects most likely to be successful?

   A Matrix structures
   B Divisional structures
   C Network structures
   D Entrepreneurial structures

5.3 Which of the following is a difference between line management and project management?

   A Management of staff
   B Reporting requirements
   C Clear objectives to work towards
   D The need to deal with customers and their needs

5.4 Which one of the following is not one of the nine key areas of project management per the Project Management Institute?

   A Objectives
   B Cost
   C Procurement
   D Integration

5.5 Which of the following is not a resource which project managers have to co-ordinate and manage?

   A People
   B Materials
   C Assets
   D Quality

5.6 Which of the following is a skill not always required by project managers?

   A Leadership skills
   B Communication skills
   C Marketing skills
   D Problem-solving skills

5.7 Phyllis is a project manager for an IT development project managing two staff and three major suppliers with whom contracts have been agreed, and who have begun the development work. Which of the following is the key role for Phyllis to ensure the success of the project?

   A Team structure
   B Problem-solving skills
   C Time planning and co-ordination
   D Costing and budgeting

5.8 Which of the following would not be included within scope, in the nine areas of project management?

   A Discussions with clients about their requirements
   B Agreeing objectives

C Clarifying what will not be covered by the project
D Time planning

5.9 Which of the following is NOT an objective of project management?

A To ensure the required standards of quality are met
B To keep all stakeholders engaged and ensure their needs are met
C To complete the project on time
D To keep ongoing operations on track with clearly organised tasks

5.10 A local authority have a project to renovate their canteen and its facilities. Which of the following is a key stakeholder in this project?

A The local authority staff
B The local public
C National Government
D The authorities' IT supplier

5.11 In which of the following organisational structures is project-based working likely to be culturally the norm?

A Simple
B Divisional
C Network
D Matrix

5.12 Which of the following is the most important skill required by a project manager?

A Writing skills
B Communication
C Marketing skills
D Financial management

5.13 Which of the following is not a project?

A Building a bridge
B Producing the monthly management accounts
C An office move
D Developing a new IT system

5.14 Complete the gaps in this definition of project management from the Association of Project Managers:

"A human activity that achieves a clear _____ against a _____"

(2 marks)

5.15 Which 2 of the following are not primarily the role of the project manager:

- Managing staff
- Negotiating with suppliers
- Staff appraisals
- Oiling the political wheels to facilitate the project's progress
- Scoping the project
- Making the project plan
- Undertaking project activities

(2 marks)

✓ Knowledge test – Answers

5.1 D

The project board is a group of people tasked with overseeing the project. They meet periodically when progress is reported to them, and have authority delegated to them by the project sponsor to allow significant project changes. The project sponsor provides overall resources and makes the investment decision.

The project manager is responsible for planning and day-to-day management of the project. The project champion is a senior person who supports the project to aid its success.

5.2 A

A matrix structure is often set up to allow for the creation of new project teams as is necessary for the business. Staff are likely to have the appropriate team-working skills and project experience. Internal processes are likely to allow for new projects to be set up and resourced easily.

5.3 D

All project management is undertaken on behalf of either internal or external customers. Although line management may include dealing with customers, many line management tasks are internally focused with no customer in mind. A-C are common to both line and project management.

5.4 A

The nine areas are Integration, Scope, Time, Cost, Quality, Risk, Procurement, Resources and Communication.

5.5 D

People, materials and assets are resources, quality is not a resource, although through co-ordinating and managing resources the project manager has quality targets.

5.6 C

Although the project manager may occasionally have to market an end product to customers, and may be involved in selling the project to customers in the first instance, this is often not the case. Leadership, communication and problem solving are always undertaken by project managers.

5.7 C

In this project, the majority of the work is being undertaken by external contractors. Costs are likely to have been agreed in the supplier's contracts so are unlikely to be important. Most of the problem solving will be done by the contractors, and the team is small so its structure is unimportant. Of great importance though is managing and monitoring the suppliers and ensuring that they are working effectively together where their work overlaps. Time planning and co-ordination are therefore a very important element of this.

5.8 D

Time planning is covered by the "time" area. Although timing objectives would be included in the scoping of the project, detailed planning of resources would not.

Introduction to Project Management

5.9 **D**

Ongoing operations are not projects, so not a purpose of project management.

5.10 **A**

The local authorities' staff are a key stakeholder as the end-users of the project. Ultimately it is their needs which must be met by the project. The IT supplier could have some minor role, perhaps in systems for purchasing supplies.

5.11 **D**

Matrix organisations have a structure and internal systems which naturally allow for new projects to start up. As well as working in their functional or divisional group, people are part of another team with some clear task focus. This team often works on a project-by-project basis.

5.12 **B**

All are important, but B is the most crucial role of project managers, communicating and coordinating the various project stakeholders.

5.13 **B**

Projects are typically thought of as being one-off, apart from 'business as usual', whereas, producing monthly management accounts is something which is regularly repeated and will have a set process and team to do it, which is the same month by month.

5.14 "A human activity that achieves a clear <u>objective</u> against a <u>timescale</u>"

5.15
- Oiling the political wheels to facilitate the project's progress – normally undertaken by the project champion.
- Undertaking project activities – although the project manager may get involved in project activities, this is primarily the role of the project team.

The Project Management Process

The Project Management Process

6

The project life cycle – the 4-D model

Maylor outlined four discreet stages in the life of a project. Any well-controlled project should plan to go through each.

Define the project

Initiation	The project is conceived and its overriding purpose set down.
Formation	The project team is selected and their roles and responsibilities defined. Resources such as a budget, rooms, computers and so on are allocated to the team so they can properly undertake their work.
Objectives	An outline of the objectives of the project (what will be achieved and by when) is created.
Feasibility study	The aim of the feasibility study is to prevent unfeasible projects to progress beyond the planning stage wasting both time and money. Key risks are identified and consideration given as to how these risks can be managed.

Feasibility is usually examined using the following categories:

- Business (meets business needs)
- Economic (costs vs benefits, NPV, IRR, payback period)
- Social (effects on people such as motivation)
- Technical (technically possible and suitable).

Design the project

Fact finding	Interviews, questionnaires and research are undertaken to clarify project details, understand exactly what the client wants, and assess potential problems.

Position analysis (SWOT analysis)	The results of the fact-finding exercise are summarised in a position analysis. This examines the project's Strengths and Weaknesses (which come from internal factors like the team and their resources) and Opportunities and Threats (which come from factors external to the project like company policy changes).
Options generation	The possible approaches to achieving the objectives are outlined.
Options evaluation	These options are evaluated in relation to the position analysis and a decision made of how the project will proceed.
Task planning	Project plan defined.
Justification	Costs vs benefits outlined based on final plan.
Agreement	Final agreement to proceed obtained from sponsor.

Deliver the project

Start-up	Assemble the resources and people to undertake the project.
Execute	Undertaking the planned activities.
Completion	This involves closing down the project. This might include tasks such as returning equipment, clearing project room, staff appraisals and paying any final bills.
Handover	Outcome passed to users/client.

Develop the process

Review	Review the project and how it progressed, and whether it achieved the objectives of stakeholders.
Feedback	Document lessons learnt and report these to the sponsor, ready to incorporate into future projects.

PRINCE 2

PRINCE 2 is a standardised approach to the project management process. PRINCE stands for "PRojects IN Controlled Environments". It is the UK Government's approach to project management and is regularly used by other governments and private companies.

PRINCE 2 starts after the project's initiation, project feasibility and options generation stages of the project life cycle. It takes the view that the contract to go ahead has been agreed and that the project now needs organising and controlling.

PRINCE 2 has eight processes which require managing. These are as follows:

1. Starting up a project (SU)

    - Intended to be of short duration
    - Defines responsibilities and roles
    - Appointing a project board and project manager
    - Designing a project management team
    - Preparing a project brief, including initial Business Case which provides justification for the project
    - Defining project approach
    - Planning the next stage (the initiation stage).

The output of this stage is the *initiation stage plan* which summarises all the work done at this stage.

2. Initiating the project

    - Planning quality
    - Planning the project – Detailed planning including breaking the project up into stages
    - Refine business case based on more detailed analysis and planning
    - Set up project files (e.g. quality log, lessons learned report, issue log).

    The output is a *project initiation document.* Unlike the business case, this does not change. It is a detailed project plan, with clear objectives, against which project progress is measured.

3. Directing a project

    This is the role of the project board. The project manager will report to the board who will

    - authorise the project to go ahead
    - authorise stage plans as the project progresses
    - give ad hoc direction (e.g. where problems occur) and authorise changes to plans
    - confirm project closure.

4. Controlling a stage

    Projects are divided into manageable stages to ensure the project remains well controlled. The number of stages will depend on the size of the project and the level of risk. Each project stage must be completed before starting the next and each new stage is planned in the stage proceeding it. It is managed by the project manager. Controlling a stage includes

    - assessing progress
    - capturing and examining key issues, and taking corrective action
    - reporting highlights to the project board
    - checking the output matches the product description.

5. Managing project delivery

    All outputs from a project are called products. The project manager clearly specifies products and manages their production and delivery by the team or external suppliers.

6. Managing stage boundaries

    At the end of each stage the project's progress will be reviewed. Lessons are learnt and incorporated into the next stage. Managing stage boundaries includes

    - updating the overall project plan
    - updating the business case
    - updating the risk log
    - producing an exception plan (caused by the project not meeting planned costs, quality targets or time plans)
    - reporting stage end to the board who authorise the project to progress to the next stage
    - planning the next stage.

7. Closing a project

    Closing the project ensures a clear end to the project, which prevents the project drifting into operational management, and provides an opportunity to celebrate achievement and learn lessons for future projects. Closing a project involves

- agreeing with customers and suppliers that the project is completed
- notifying stakeholders of project completion
- formal handover of "products" to client
- document follow-action recommendations
- plan the Post Project Review (which evaluates the benefits outlined in the business case, the quality of management and identifies the lessons learnt)
- conduct the Post Project Review.

8. Planning

    Planning occurs throughout the project, and is a constituent of many other processes as well as being defined as a process in its own right. Planning includes

    - defining the product and writing a product description
    - identifying activities and dependencies
    - estimating (timescales, costs, capabilities)
    - scheduling (what and when)
    - analysing risks and making contingency plans
    - completing a plan – including authorisation of the plan by the board.

Implications for project staff of PRINCE 2

In PRINCE 2 the project manager is charged with managing the project within the constraints imposed by the project board. For anything outside the scope of that agreed with the board, the project manager must gain approval from the board. There is therefore a clearly defined relationship between the board and project manager. The project manager must follow a restricted step-by-step procedure following all eight processes and the many sub-processes within them.

Project staff must operate under a strictly managed and controlled regime. They must ensure that what they are doing is within the bounds of agreed project objectives and scope as outlined in the business case, and is consistent with the business plans.

Maylor's 7-S model

This model was originally developed by McKinsey for use in organisations as a whole. It was later adapted by Maylor to be applicable for project management and outlines seven key areas which should be considered in the development of projects.

The 3S's across the top of the model are described as "Hard S's". These are clear, tangible areas to be addressed.

Strategy	The direction and scope of the project.
Structure	How the project is organised – roles and responsibilities.
Systems	Formal and informal procedures that govern project activity, for example use of standardised approach like PRINCE 2.

The 4S's across the bottom of the model are less tangible, more cultural in nature, and were termed "Soft S's" by McKinsey:

Staff	The project team, their skills and mix of personalities.
Style	The management style and approach of the project director or manager and culture within the group.

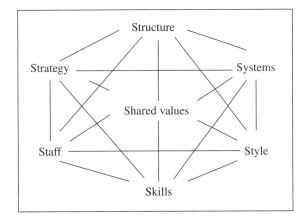

Stakeholders   Those people with an interest in, or power over, the project.
Skills   The skills and resources needed for successful completion of the project.

Knowledge test – Quick questions

6.1 In PRINCE 2 how many process are there?

    A 5
    B 6
    C 8
    D 10

6.2 In PRINCE 2 which of the following is included in managing stage boundaries?

    A Motivating the project team
    B Updating the project initiation document
    C Undertaking stage activities
    D Reviewing the project against objectives and updating the project plan

6.3 In PRINCE 2 which of the following is not a process?

    A Planning
    B Managing stage boundaries
    C Directing
    D Authorising

6.4 Which of the following is not a stage in the 4-D project life cycle?

    A Delivery
    B Design
    C Development
    D Draw to a close

6.5 Which of the following is not a benefit of using PRINCE 2?

    A Well-controlled project
    B Behavioural change processes are considered
    C Tried and tested approach to projects
    D Clear stages to progress through creating specific milestones

6.6 Which of the following would not be included in the Deliver stage of the 4-D approach?

  A Changing the project plan for changing circumstances
  B SWOT analysis
  C Undertaking project activities
  D Handover to client

6.7 In Maylor's 7-S model, which of the following are not a hard factor?

  A Skills
  B Systems
  C Strategy
  D Structure

6.8 Which of the following is not included within the Design stage of the project life cycle?

  A Scoping the project
  B Options appraisal
  C Position analysis
  D Options generation

6.9 In which of the following is PRINCE 2 least likely to be used?

  A Development of a new IT system
  B A road construction project
  C An office move
  D Managing the recruitment process for new staff

6.10 In PRINCE 2, planning occurs at what stage of the project?

  A At the start
  B After initiating the project
  C During the project delivery stage
  D Throughout the project

6.11 The style element of McKinsey's 7-S model includes which of the following:

  A IT systems
  B The way managers manage their team
  C The way people learn
  D The approach to strategy

6.12 Which of the following is not a key element of the project management triangle?

  A Quality
  B Cost
  C Time
  D People

6.13 Complete the gaps. PRINCE 2 stands for:

  Projects IN _____ _____ 2   **(2 marks)**

6.14 Briefly explain the 3 hard S's in Maylor's 7-S model   **(3 marks)**

Knowledge test – Answers

6.1 **C**

PRINCE 2 has eight processes:

1. Starting up a project (SU)
2. Initiating the project
3. Directing a project
4. Controlling a stage
5. Managing project delivery
6. Managing stage boundaries
7. Closing a project
8. Planning.

6.2 **D**

The business case may be changed as the project progresses through its stages, but the project initiation document stays the same. Managing stage boundaries includes

- updating the overall project plan
- updating the business case
- updating the risk log
- producing an exception plan (caused by the project not meeting planned costs, quality targets or time plans)
- reporting stage end to the board who authorise the project to progress to the next stage
- planning the next stage.

6.3 **D**

All others are processes in the PRINCE 2 process.

6.4 **D**

The stages are: Define, Design, Deliver, Development.

6.5 **B**

PRINCE 2 gives a tried and tested approach to projects which ensures projects are well controlled. PRINCE 2 ensures the project is broken down into stages at the end of which a review may be undertaken and the project board authority sought to pass to the next stage. PRINCE 2 does not incorporate a behavioural change approach into the methodology.

6.6 **B**

The delivery stage includes putting the project team and resources together, implementing the project, completing the project and handing it over to the client. A SWOT analysis would be conducted as part of the design stage to help to understand the project's current position and plan activities based on this.

6.7 **A**

Skills is a soft factor, all the others are hard factors that is, clearly definable and straightforward to change.

6.8 **A**

The Design stage includes Planning, Fact finding, Position analysis, Options generation and Options evaluation. Scoping of the project is undertaken in the defining stage.

6.9 **D**

PRINCE 2 tends to be used on larger projects where there is a lot to organise and control like the new IT system or road construction project. It could be used for an office move although might be considered a little over-bureaucratic. It is least likely to be used in managing the recruitment process which is likely to have a standardised process set down, and is more part of ongoing operations.

6.10 **D**

Planning occurs throughout the project and is a constituent of many of the processes as well as being defined as a PRINCE 2 process in its own right.

6.11 **B**

Style is concerned with the management style used by managers when managing staff (e.g. autocratic or democratic).

6.12 **D**

The project management triangle says that there are 3 key inter-related elements of a project, quality, cost and time. As one of these changes, it will inevitably effect the others. For instance, if timescales are reduced quality may need to be sacrificed, and costs are likely to change, for example to pay staff overtime to complete quickly.

6.13 Projects IN Controlled Environments 2

6.14 The Hard S's are the clear, tangible elements in an organisation's culture. They are

1. *Strategy* – This sets out the direction and scope and how success will be achieved.
2. *Structure* – This is how roles and responsibilities are allocated to achieve the organisation's or project's goals.
3. *Systems* – The procedures in place which govern how activities are undertaken either in the organisation or the project. They can include both manual and information systems.

Project Planning

Project Planning 7

Project plans

Project plans are intended to organise, manage and control projects by outlining objectives and how those objectives will be achieved, taking into consideration possible problems that may arise.

A good project plan will include the following:

- executive summary – provides an overview of all other sections
- project quality plan
- clearly defined scope
- project objectives, milestones and gates
- key assumptions
- methodology that will be used (e.g. PRINCE 2)
- technical details
- time plan (e.g. network diagram, Gantt chart)
- communication plan
- people (numbers, skills, key personnel, hierarchy, organisation, roles)
- other resourcing issues
- budget
- monitoring process.

The time/cost/quality trade-off

One key aspect of planning is balancing the trade-off between time, cost and quality. For example,

- Allowing more time for the project will tend to increase the quality as the project team can spend longer perfecting the output. On the downside it is also likely to increase costs for staff and resource usage.
- Setting higher quality standards may necessitate higher costs, since better qualified staff might be used, more expensive suppliers required and higher quality materials and assets needed. It could also increase timescales as people require longer to perfect the project output.

When planning, the project manager must balance the consequences of each of these in order to ensure that targets for quality, timescale and cost are all hit.

It may be that one of these dimensions takes priority over others. In preparing for Olympic Games, time is the highest priority since this is immovable. If developing a banking system for processing transactions, quality would be the most important dimension, since even small errors are not acceptable.

Project scope

Achieving quality, time and cost targets, means setting achievable targets at the start of the project while also ensuring that the clients' needs are met. This will mean

- Discussions with stakeholders about project expectations (quality, time, cost). This might be done using interviews, questionnaires or group meetings.
- Agreeing output and costs with the client.
- Negotiating for suitable resources with the project board.
- Initial discussions with suppliers of likely timescales and costs.

Risk management

An analysis of the possible risks should be undertaken at the start of the project. This includes examining

(a) Possible risks:

Quantitative	Can be expressed in a financial amount.
Qualitative	Other risks which cannot be quantified.
Socially constructed	Risks in the minds of users/clients which evidence shows are unlikely to occur, but need to be managed to ensure people's expectations are managed.

(b) Likelihood of threat occurring
(c) Possible downside impact
(d) How risks will be handled:

Avoidance
- leave risk with customer
- do not undertake risky elements of the project.

Transference
- subcontract so supplier takes risk
- insure.

Reduction
- use reliable /experienced suppliers
- use skilled staff
- secure more time or resources
- making contingency plans (e.g. maintain links with alternative suppliers).

Evaluating plans

One of the key syllabus requirements is to be able to evaluate plans. You will notice that much of the content of a good plan can be summarised by relating the plan to the nine key project areas outlined in Chapter 5. This can therefore be a useful model to use to evaluate project plans. The following table outlines some of the key questions which can be used in the evaluation.

Nine key areas	Evaluating project plans
Integration	Has planning been undertaken? Are plans based on detailed analysis and research? Have any methodologies to be used been outlined? Have change management issues been considered?
Scope	Has time been allocated to properly scope out the project? Is the scope based on discussions with all key stakeholders? Have objectives been specified? Are objectives SMART (**S**pecific, **M**easurable, **A**chievable, **R**elevant, **T**ime bound)?
Time	Have time-planning models been used (e.g. Gantt charts, Network diagrams)? Have critical activities been identified and prioritised? Are timings realistic? Has uncertainty been allowed for in the time plan? All key activities have been identified (possibly using a Work Breakdown Structure).
Cost	Has a budget been set? Is it realistic? Is it based on a detailed analysis of project activities/tasks? Has cost monitoring and control been planned for?
Quality	Has a Project Quality Plan been set out? How will quality be monitored and controlled? How will quality be assured?
Resources	Resources identified for all key activities? Has a resource histogram been used to plan resource requirements? Have sufficient resources been planned for? Is there the budget to acquire these resources? Are they available (e.g. properly skilled staff)?
Communication	How will plans be communicated to the team? Have regular reporting to project board/sponsor/owner/client been included? How will other stakeholders be kept informed of project progress?
Risk	Have key risks been identified? Have plans to mitigate or eliminate these risks been made? Have key assumptions been stated? Is suitable insurance in place? Are suitable contingency plans in place?
Procurement	Are plans in place to evaluate the suitability, reliability and financial strength of suppliers?

Project planning tools

Work breakdown structure

This is a technique used to identify the tasks involved in the project. At the top level, the whole project is broken down into the main project elements. At the next level, each element is then broken down into the individual tasks involved to complete that. Each of these tasks is then broken down into smaller parts. This process continues until tasks can no longer be reasonably broken down further.

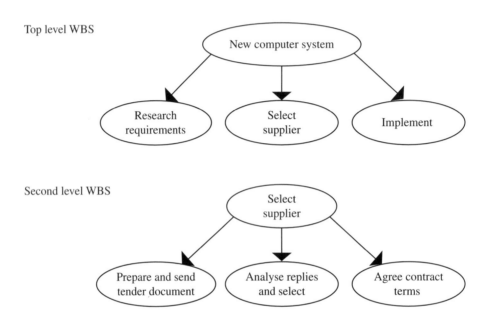

This is an important way of assessing the resources required by the project. The work breakdown structure can be used to estimate:

(a) Likely timings of tasks so a project plan can be defined.
(b) Numbers of people, machinery, materials and so on required at different stages.
(c) Project costs using a cost breakdown structure.

This involves allocating costs to each of the smallest units and building up the costs from the lowest to the highest level.

Network analysis

Network analysis is a technique used to plan and sequence the different tasks which must be undertaken in the project. This ensures that projects are thought through and organised in the most efficient way.

Network analysis is particularly good at identifying the critical tasks – those which need to be completed on time to avoid the project being delayed.

Notation and rules for drawing a network diagram

(a) Events – The start or end of an activity. The notation used for an event is

(b) Activities – Activities are the tasks undertaken. The notation for them is an arrow joining two events.

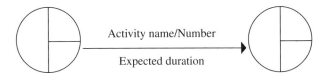

(c) The steps in drawing a network diagram are

   1. On the left of the page, draw the starting event (there must only be one start event).
   2. Look out for the following patterns in the question:

      - Where an activity must be followed by two (or more) activities. At these points, the diagram will look like this

      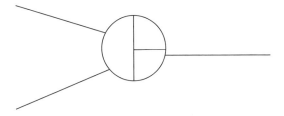

      - Where one activity must be preceded by two (or more) activities. At these points, the diagram will look like this

      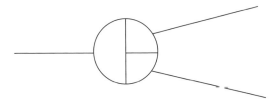

   3. Draw the activities and events from left to right:

      - there must be no loops or crossed lines
      - no two activities may share the same head and tail event, that is, the following is not allowed

      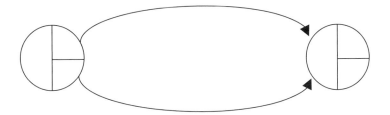

- instead dummy activities are used. These have zero duration and run from the earliest to the latest event.

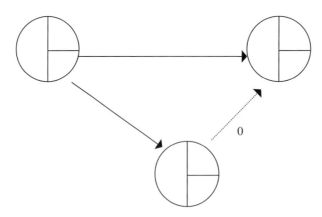

4. There must be only one end event – on the right hand side of the diagram.
5. In time order (earliest to latest), number the events in the left hand semi-circle of the event.

6. Calculate the earliest event time for each event (the earliest time it is possible to get to that event) from left to right. Where there are two options take the higher number.

7. Calculate the latest event time (the latest an event can start and not delay the project) from right to left. Where there are two options take the lower number.

8. Note the critical path (by following the diagram from left to right following the route where the LET = EET).

The critical path shows the activities which must finish on time if the project as a whole is to be completed on time. Identifying the critical path allows resources to be allocated to these activities and provides focus to the project managers monitoring activities.

Example of a network diagram

Activity	Description	Duration (weeks)	Preceded by
A	Planning	2	–
B	Recruit project team	3	–
C	Design	2	A,B
D	Training course development	4	B
E	Implementation	5	C
F	Training users	4	D

This system would produce the following network diagram.

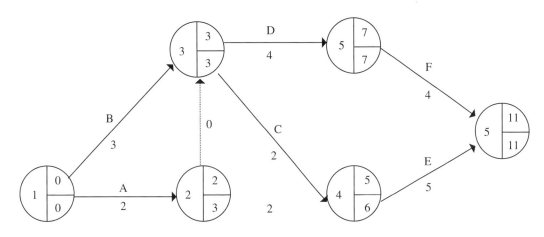

Critical path – B D F

Gantt charts

Gantt charts are a technique used to plan and sequence the different project tasks. Gantt charts use a simple bar chart format with the bars representing the length of each task.

Developing a new computer system	
Task	Time (weeks) 1 2 3 4 5 6 7 8 9 10 11 12 13 14 15 16
(1) Set up team	
(2) User discussion	
(3) Select possible suppliers	
(4) Prepare and send out tender document	
(5) Collate and examine replies	
(6) Choose supplier	
(7) System development	
(8) System implementation	
(9) Staff training	

▢ Plan

▨ Actual

In the above Gantt chart, the project is currently near the end of Week 11. The project started off as planned. However, the selection of suppliers took two weeks longer than expected. This has delayed all subsequent activities and the project now appears to be two weeks behind schedule.

Advantages of Gantt charts compared with network diagrams
1. Good communication tool, since they are easy to understand and produce a useful visual summary.
2. Easy to create.

Disadvantages of Gantt charts compared with network diagrams
1. Critical activities are not identified.
2. Not clear which activities must be completed before other activities begin.
3. For complex projects with many activities the chart becomes large and loses its benefit as a communication tool.

Resource histograms

Neither Gantt charts nor network diagrams consider the resources required by a project. To do this a resource histogram can be used. This shows graphically the resources required over the term of the project.

Example of a resource histogram

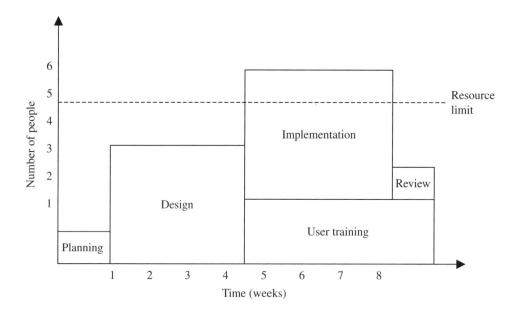

This resource histogram clearly shows that given the team size of five people that there will not be enough people between Weeks 4 and 7. This alerts the project manager of the potential problem and allows them to find ways of overcoming the resourcing issue. In this case the project manager might consider:

- Reducing design time to three weeks to use the spare resource better in this time, and starting implementation early.
- Extending the implementation phase by a week and using fewer people. This will delay the whole project by a week.
- Applying for extra resources for Weeks 4–7.

Gates and milestones

Often projects have clear stages, for example, the end of design and start of implementation, or the completion of planning and the beginning of development. Milestones are the end points of these stages at which there may be a "gate".

To pass through a "gate" a set of pre-defined criteria must be met in order for the project to proceed form one stage to the next. This will typically involve a checklist of deliverables which indicate the state of completion of each item. Approval may be required from the project board for the project to proceed.

Reaching a milestone may also signify payments from customers.

Dealing with uncertainty

PERT (Project Evaluation and Review Technique)

PERT is a way of considering uncertainty in projects. Rather than simply estimating one time estimate, three are estimated. These being a

- pessimistic estimate (p)
- expected estimate (m)
- optimistic estimate (o).

Using these estimates an average can be found using the formula:

$$\frac{p + 4m + o}{6}$$

This average can then be used to create a revised Network diagram or Gantt chart.

Scenario planning

In scenario planning a project manager will review possible different occurrences which might arise, by asking a series of what if questions.

For example, what if

- a supplier went bust
- a key delivery was delayed
- our budget got cut
- a key member of staff left.

This allows the project manager to

- make contingency plans where consequences are significant and probable
- allocate more resources to risky areas
- calculate more accurate estimates for the PERT analysis
- monitor key risk areas more closely to ensure problems do not occur.

Buffering

Buffering is the allowance of extra time in the project timeline to account for uncertainties and unexpected events. Buffering helps to ensure that project deadlines can be met and hence client expectations managed.

Project management software

Most of the project management tools are now performed using project management software (e.g. Microsoft Project). This automates the process and allows

- quick and easy creation of project plans
- more accurate project planning
- easy "what if" analysis (scenario planning) to be undertaken
- budgeting to be connected to plans
- progress to be monitored and updates easily made
- reports to be produced (e.g. progress reports, financial reports), useful for communication purposes.

❓ Knowledge test – Quick questions

7.1 Examining the Gantt chart below, which of the following statements is not true?

   A The project length is 22 weeks.
   B The first task took longer than expected.
   C Task 3 was delayed.
   D The project is currently in Week 17.

7.2 Using the Gantt chart in Question 7.1, which of the following is definitely true?

   A Task 6 was poorly planned.
   B Task 7 has not been completed.
   C Task 2 cannot be completed before Task 1 is finished.
   D Task 8 has yet to be started.

7.3 A project has a strict deadline demanded by the client. The project manager has only a small team of staff who have client-specific knowledge who can work on the project. There is not enough time to train new staff in at such short notice. Tasks do not have to be undertaken in any specific order. Given the resource histogram below, what might be a solution to the project manager's problem?

   A Delay Task 2 by one week.
   B Extend both Tasks 1 and 4 by one week, and begin Task 4 earlier.
   C Use temporary staff from an agency in Weeks 1, 3 and 4.
   D Delay the project by a few weeks and extend all activities, spreading resources more evenly.

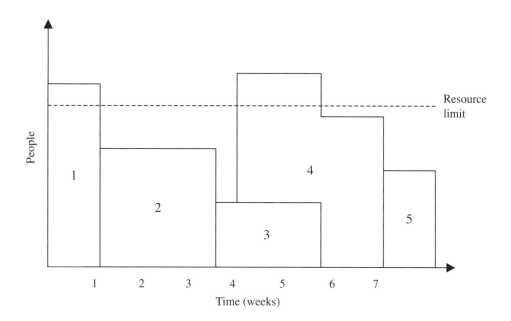

7.4 In the scenario from Question 7.3. Which of the following is not necessarily true?

   A Task 5 represents the completion stage.
   B The resourcing limit is exceeded in Weeks 1, 3 and 4.
   C Tasks 3 and 4 can be carried out simultaneously.
   D The project has a duration of seven weeks.

7.5 A socially constructed risk can be defined by which of the following statements?

   A A risk caused by uncertainties inherent in dealing with people.
   B A risk related to communication.
   C A risk in the minds of people which does not necessarily have a basis in reality.
   D The risk to the local people in a building project.

7.6 Which of the following do not represent ways of managing risk?

A Transference
B Allowance
C Reduction
D Avoidance

7.7 Which of the following would not be included in a project plan?

A Gantt chart
B Quality plan
C Contingency arrangements
D Project designs

7.8 Which of the following is an advantage of a network chart compared with a Gantt chart?

A Better communication tool to the project's stakeholders.
B Clearly shows the activities which must be completed on time for the project and not to be delayed.
C Easier to complete.
D Clearly shows planned and actual results.

7.9 Considering the time/cost/quality trade-off, allowing more time for the project causes

A Cost increases, quality increases
B Cost decreases, quality increases
C Cost decreases, quality decreases
D Cost increases, quality decreases

7.10 Which of the following would NOT normally be found in a project plan?

A Time plan
B Communication plan
C People (numbers, skills, key personnel, hierarchy, organisation, roles)
D The company's organisational chart

7.11 Socially contructed risk is

A The financial risk
B General risks identified by staff and other stakeholers
C Risks that staff believe to be true (although they may not indeed be in reality)
D Cultural risk

7.12 Which of the following is not a project management tool or technique?

A Work Breakdown structure
B Network analysis
C PERT
D Value chain analysis

7.13 Explain 3 benefits of having a project plan. **(3 marks)**

7.14 Briefly explain 3 ways to manage risk. **(3 marks)**

Knowledge test – Answers

7.1 **D**

The project is currently in Week 19. Task 3 took the same time as expected, but was delayed by approximately one week.

7.2 **D**

- A Although Task 6 was undertaken at a different time than expected, it does not necessarily mean it was poorly planned. Circumstances could have changed which allowed it to be done early.
- B Task 7 has probably not been completed, but it is possible that it has just been completed (e.g. through allocating more resources to it).
- C Both the plan and actual results suggest that Task 2 does follow Task 1. However this does not have to be true, it may simply be the way the project was planned. An advantage of network analysis is that this relationship would be clear.
- D Definitely true since there is no actual bar for this task.

7.3 **B**

- A The resourcing problem is Weeks 1, 3 and 4. Delaying Task 2 makes no difference.
- B Corrects the problem and the project deadlines will still be achieved.
- C Temporary staff will not be suitable since they are unlikely to have the necessary client knowledge.
- D Unlikely to be acceptable to the client, given the strict deadlines.

7.4 **A**

Task 5 is unlikely to be the project completion stage since all tasks can be completed in any order and the project completion stage will always be at the end of the project.

7.5 **C**

All other answers are made up and therefore incorrect.

7.6 **B**

- A Transference means giving the risk to another party such as a subcontractor or insurer.
- C Reducing risk means accepting that some risks will be incurred but aiming to keep the likelihood of the risk occurring to a minimum, or if it does then minimising the negative consequences. For example, using reliable/experienced suppliers or making contingency plans.
- D Avoiding the risk could mean leaving risk with customer or not undertaking risky elements of the project.

7.7 **D**

Example of project designs could include the design of an IT system or building designs. These will be undertaken as part of the execution stage of the project process. All other answers could be found in a project plan.

7.8 **B**

One key advantage of network charts is that you can use them to identify the critical path. Each activity on the critical path must be completed on time or the whole project will be delayed. All other answers are advantages of Gantt charts over Network charts.

7.9 **A**

Allowing more time for the project will tend to increase the quality as the project team can spend longer perfecting the output. On the downside it is also likely to increase costs for staff and resource usage.

7.10 **D**

You are unlikely to find an organisational chart, detailing the structure of the organisation, for the whole organisation in the project plan. Such a chart for the project is likely to be included.

7.11 **C**

Socially constructed risks are risks in the minds of users/clients which, evidence shows, are unlikely to occur, but need to be managed to ensure people's expectations are managed.

7.12 **D**

PERT stands for Project Evaluation Review Technique and allows for flexibility to be built into time management of projects. Value chain analysis is a model used to examine the value added in a number of key activities of the business and is used in strategic analysis not projects.

7.13
1. The project should be finished within the expected timescale by calculating timings for various activities, monitoring progress throughout and taking control action where activities are behind plan.
2. Setting quality standards and planning how these will be achieved in the Project Quality Plan ensures the required quality is clear and will be achieved.
3. Cost overruns should be reduced since activities as a result of time overruns being reduced and pre-planning of how cost targets will be achieved.

7.14
1. *Avoidance* – do not undertake highly risky projects or elements of the project
2. *Transference* – passing the risk on to another party (e.g. insurance)
3. *Reduction* – reducing the likelihood of the risk happening.

Executing and Completing Projects

Executing and Completing Projects

8

Allowing for change during a project

As the project progresses, project plans should be updated and changes passed to the team.

Regular communication of progress and changes to plans is a common part of project working to ensure the project progresses in an efficient manner. Project management software makes the monitoring process easy, as new project plans can be drawn up quickly and efficiently.

A formal *project change procedure* may be put in place to ensure

(a) major project changes are authorised
(b) only appropriate changes are made
(c) new plans are communicated to all stakeholders.

The project manager should monitor any major threats identified in the risk assessment done at the planning stage, and where possible anticipate problems before they occur and make changes accordingly.

Controlling performance

Project not meeting objectives

Projects do not always meet their objectives. Reasons why the project might overrun, for example, can include

(a) changing objectives
(b) risks not clearly identified and dealt with at the scoping stage
(c) insufficient budget
(d) poor planning
(e) unrealistic deadlines
(f) resources are not available
(g) poor quality resources used (staff, suppliers, equipment)
(h) unclear project structure
(i) the required standards of quality are not met and reworking is required.

Performance management

The aim of performance management is to ensure, as far as possible, that the project meets its objectives. Performance management involves a three stage process:

(i) Set objectives (e.g. to complete the project within a budget of £4m)
(ii) Monitor progress (e.g. measure the current cost position)
(iii) Take control action (e.g. use cheaper materials/suppliers to cut costs).

Throughout the project's life, the project manager will review performance against targets and milestones and make changes which will keep the project on track.

Where the project is not on track and remedial action is unlikely to achieve the target, the project manager should first inform the project board, who may authorise changes such as increased resources and/or the client.

Conformance management

Conformance management involves ensuring that the project team and suppliers conform to agreed standards and protocols. Like performance management this aims to ensure the project is well controlled and thus meets its objectives.

This might, for instance, involve ensuring that suppliers deliver products or services according to agreed timescales, and will involve setting standards and reviewing supplier progress.

Earned value management

Earned value management (EVM) aids project management by providing a financial measure of project progress, based on the actual amount of work undertaken. Standard project management measurement usually uses a range of individual measurement criteria in areas such as scope, time and costs. The key difference of EVM is that it allows for these different elements to be *combined in a single financial measure*.

Elements of EVM
Project plan
This sets out the list of activities being undertaken along with expected timescales.

A Planned Value
A planned value is the budgeted cost of works over the course of the project. The activities in the project plan are costed, and estimated times in which the money will be spent assigned so that estimated costs at particular stages of the project are calculated.

Earned Value
Standard project measurement would typically compare the budget (here called the planned value) with actual cost. In certain circumstances this can be misleading. As an example, here is a table of budgets for months 3 and 4 of a project, and the estimated percentage completion of the project at that stage:

Time	Planned value	Estimated % complete
Month 3	£10,000	50
Month 4	£14,000	60

If the actual cost of work done at the end of month 3 was £12,000, under a standard system of budget variances it would appear that the project was over budget at this stage. However, if the project was actually one month ahead of schedule and was now 60% complete, you can see that in fact costs are lower than would be expected for that level of completion of the project.

Earned value management aims to overcome this problem. A set of rules are set up at the start of the project to quantify the value of work accomplished. Often this involves assigning a value to the completion of each individual activity in the plan. During the project, earned values are calculated based on the activities actually completed and compared to planned values and actual costs in order to ascertain whether the project is on track. In this case the earned value at the end of month 3 would reflect the 60% completion (in this case roughly £14,000), and therefore would provide a more objective measure for comparison with actual cost.

Project completion

Completion activities

To complete the project the following activities must be undertaken:

- completion of project documentation
- filing project documentation so it is organised and available for future access if needed
- appraising staff
- paying all suppliers
- sign-off of deliverables with the customer/client
- collection of amounts owed from clients
- marketing the deliverables to potential users to ensure benefits are realised.

Post completion review/audit

At the end of a project, a review is undertaken so that lessons can be learnt for future projects. This may include

- team briefings
- customer debriefing
- review against project objectives (time, cost, quality)
- effectiveness of the team and project manager
- review of benefits gained by the deliverables (e.g. did the new IT system allow for a reduction in staff as expected).

Findings are summarised in a post completion report, which is presented to the project board, and used in the planning of future projects.

Project documentation

A range of documents are produced during the project's life.

Project initiation document/project charter/project brief

At the end of the defining stage, a project initiation document is produced. This is intended to provide an outline of the project and its purpose. It is approved by the project sponsor/board, giving the project manager the authority to proceed with the project. It contains details such as

- objectives
- risks
- overall budget
- resources allocated
- roles and responsibilities
- authority of the project team
- make up of the team
- stakeholders
- reporting plans.

Project quality plan

A *project quality plan* is also drawn up in the defining stage. This outlines the expected quality of outputs and how these quality targets will be achieved. In doing this it may cover key risks and how they will be overcome and processes for quality management. This is a key document, since the standards set down are used to assess the finished product.

Business case

A business case puts forward the reasoning of the project compared with expected costs. The business case must be authorised by the project board before the project can proceed. A business case is part of PRINCE 2 methodology. The business case is updated as the project proceeds.

Project plan

The project plan is the key output from the design stage of the project. Details of the project plan are outlined in Chapter 7.

Progress reports

As the project progresses, ongoing progress reports are produced and distributed to the project team and the project sponsor/board. The reports outline progress against plan and milestones and include any changes required.

Completion report

This summarises the results of the post completion review, outlining how well objectives of all stakeholders have been achieved and lessons learnt for future projects.

❓ Knowledge test – Quick questions

8.1 Which of the following would not be undertaken as part of the post completion activities?

    A Staff appraisals
    B Filing of documentation
    C Authorisation of quality plans by the project board
    D Post completion audit

8.2 Which of the following are reasons why a project might fail to meet its original objectives?

    (i)   Poorly defined objectives
    (ii) Insufficient resources allocated to the project
    (iii) Poor planning
    (iv) Poorly skilled staff used

    A (i) and (ii)
    B (i), (ii) and (iv)
    C (i), (iii) and (iv)
    D All of them

8.3 Which of the following statements best represents performance management?

    A Reviewing performance levels to ensure continuous improvement throughout the course of the project.
    B Staff assessment and appraisal.
    C Review of performance against agreed targets, and where necessary taking remedial action to ensure that performance levels are at expected levels.
    D Regular progress reviews followed by reporting to the board.

8.4 Under the PRINCE 2 stage, closing a project, which of the following would not be undertaken?

    A Final authorisation of stage plans by project board
    B Agreeing with customers and suppliers that the project is completed
    C Notifying stakeholders of project completion
    D Formal handover of "products" to client

8.5 In the project life cycle, what is the output from the planning stage?

    A Detailed project plan
    B Project initiation document
    C Business case
    D Project quality plan

8.6 Which of the following is NOT true about changes to the project?

    A Change is an inevitable part of any project
    B Under PRINCE 2, changes must be authorised by the project board
    C It is good practice for a formal change procedure to be drafted and used by the project manager when major project changes are necessary
    D Project planning software facilitates the process of project change

8.7 Project management software is useful for which of the following reasons?

    (i) Allows all project staff to quickly and easily change project plans and communicate these changes to others
    (ii) Allows creation of project plans for different scenarios to aid planning
    (iii) Facilitates production of progress reports
    (iv) Helps avoid team conflict

    A (ii) and (iii)
    B (i), (ii) and (iii)
    C (i) and (iii)
    D All of them

8.8 What is the best definition of a post completion audit?

    A A review of the project and how well it achieved its objectives, conducted after its completion in order to learn lessons for use in future projects.
    B The final team briefing which closes down the project.
    C A review of final deliverables prior to being passed over to the client.
    D A step-by-step analysis of the project's progress to understand why problems occurred.

8.9 Which of following best describes conformance management?

    A Ensuring that the project team and suppliers conform to agreed standards and protocols.
    B Ensuring as far as possible that the project meets its objectives
    C Ensuring people conform to the project plan
    D Ensuring conformance is project-managed effectively, without allowing for non-conforming parties to non-conform to the objective

8.10 Which of the following would be found in a completion report?

    A Lessons learnt from the project
    B The completed project plan
    C A resource histogram
    D A note of the projects current postion at the end of the current project stage

8.11 What would you NOT expect to see in a business case?

    A Analysis of risks
    B Objectives
    C Expected costs
    D Critical path analysis

8.12 Briefly explain 3 elements of the project initiation document. **(3 marks)**

8.13 Name 4 completion activities **(4 marks)**

Knowledge test – Answers

8.1 **C**

Quality plans are completed during the initiation and planning stages, and will be authorised by the project board at this early stage. The post completion review may include a review of the quality plans, so lessons learnt can be passed on for future projects.

8.2 **D**

8.3 **C**

Performance management ensures that supplier, staff and project performance is maintained at expected levels. This may include reporting to the board, and staff assessment but these are just parts of the performance management process.

8.4 **A**

Under PRINCE 2, the project is broken up into stages. Stage plans made and authorised at the beginning of each stage. PRINCE 2 includes a process called "Managing stage boundaries" in which stage plans are finalised. All other activities above are undertaken in the "Closing a Project" stage.

8.5 **A**

The project initiation document, project quality plan and business case are most likely to be produced at the end of the initiation stage.

8.6 **B**

Under PRINCE 2 all major project changes will require authorisation by the project board. Minor changes which result during normal day-to-day operation of the project can be authorised by the project manager. All the other answers are true.

8.7 **A**

Although project management software does allow project plans to be updated quickly and easily, changes should primarily be controlled by the project manager. Team conflict usually occurs because of personal differences. Although a well-designed project plan may help avoid this, it is likely to be achieved by the project manager, considering behavioural issues during planning rather than anything the software does.

8.8 **A**

The post project review examines all aspects of the project so that lessons can be learnt for use in future projects.

8.9 **A**

Conformance management involves ensuring that the project team and suppliers conform to agreed standards and protocols. Like performance management this aims to ensure the project is well controlled and thus meets its objectives. This might, for instance, involve ensuring that suppliers deliver products or services according to agreed timescales, and will involve setting standards and reviewing supplier progress. B describes performance management. C is incorrect and D is just gobbledygook.

8.10 **A**

A completion report summarises the results of the post-completion review, outlining how well objectives of all stakeholders have been achieved and lessons learnt for future projects.

8.11 **D**

A business case puts the case for the project, justifying the expenditure and the reason why it should go ahead. Planning documentation such as a network chart is unlikely to be included at this stage.

8.12 1. *Objectives* – Give a clear target to move towards and guide the project.
2. *Risks* – Identifies risks and how these will be managed.
3. *Budget* – Outlines the overall costs and breaks these down into different areas of the project to allow for cost management.

8.13 1. Complete project documentation
2. Filing documentation
3. Appraising staff
4. Paying suppliers.

Introduction to Management Theory Leadership

Introduction to Management Theory Leadership 9

Power, authority, responsibility and delegation

Power

Power is the ability to exert influence. This may be due to the position of the individual in the organisation (i.e. their authority) but can also be due to other factors such as their ability to influence the reward (pay/promotion), their expertise, to exert punishment or due to their charisma.

Authority

Authority is the right to exert influence. A person's position in an organisation gives them authority over others. They have the right to tell those individuals what to do.

Responsibility

Responsibility gives someone the charge over or control over something. The person to whom responsibility has been assigned is the person who is in control of ensuring the task is completed, even if they delegate the completion of the task to someone else.

Delegation

Delegation is where tasks or decisions are passed to another member of staff (usually lower in the organisational hierarchy). Usually this does not involve passing over of responsibility, so although the task is delegated ultimate responsibility for getting the job done remains with the person doing the delegation.

Leadership

Leadership is the process of influencing others, to work willingly towards goals to the best of their capabilities, perhaps in a manner different to that which they would have otherwise chosen.

Personality trait theories

These theories attempt to identify the distinguishing characteristics of successful leaders. These include

- *Intelligence* – above average
- *Initiative* – independence and inventiveness
- *Self-assurance* – self-confidence
- *The helicopter factor* – the ability to see a situation in context.

Characteristics of managers and entrepreneurs

These theories assume that individuals will work harder for managers who employ different styles of leadership. Several theories of leadership are based around the question of management style.

Management styles

Likert
Likert identified four styles of management:

1. *Exploitative authoritative* – manager makes decision and enforces it
2. *Benevolent authoritative* – manager makes decision and sells it
3. *Consultative* – manager asks for suggestions on what he should decide
4. *Participative* – staff participate in decisions and are given flexibility to make their own decisions with the manager's support and advice.

Blake and Mouton
Two basic criteria for leadership:

1. concern for task (or production) being achieved
2. concern for people.

A high concern for the task will score 9 and a high concern for the people will also score 9.

Types of management:

- Task-orientated style (task = 9, people = 1 or 9, 1) – gets the job done but ignores people's needs.
- The Country club style (1, 9) – attentive to peoples needs but ignores the task.
- The Impoverished style (1,1) – ignores peoples and task needs.
- The Middle Road (5, 5) – adequate attention to both needs.
- The Team style (9,9) – gets the job done (task needs) and attentive to peoples needs.

Contingency theories of leadership

Takes view that there is not one most effective style but the most effective style will depend upon a combination of factors.

Adair – action-centred leadership
Effective leadership style requires bringing together the needs of:

- *Task* – objective setting, planning of tasks, allocation of responsibilities
- *Team* – team building, communication, discipline, acting as external representative
- *Individual* – coaching, counselling, motivation and development.

Fiedler
The most effective leadership style depends on the situation they find themselves. The situation can be defined by a combination of three factors:

1. leader and members relations
2. task structure
3. leader's power position.

Fiedler's conclusions were

- A distant style is effective when situations are very favourable or unfavourable.
- A close style works best when the situations are not extreme.

Bureaucracy (late nineteenth century and early twentieth century)

"Bureaucracy" is a term most commonly used to decide a hierarchical rule-bound organisation. It was first described in detail by Weber.

Weber's eight characteristics of a bureaucracy
1. *Specialisation* – clear division of labour
2. *Hierarchy* – a hierarchy of offices, in which offices are linked through a clear chain of command
3. *Rules* – strict rules and procedures
4. *Impersonality* – objective and rational decisions rather than personal preferences
5. *Appointed officials* – managers are selected by qualification, education or training
6. *Career officials* – managers pursue careers within the bureaucracy and work within a defined salary structure
7. *Full-time officials* – committed professionals
8. *Public/private division* – separation of officials from ownership of the organisation.

? Knowledge test – Quick questions

9.1 Recent developments towards greater employee involvement, flexible working and flatter organisational structures have placed greater emphasis on which ONE of the following styles of management?

    A   Exploitative authoritative
    B   Autocratic

C Participative
D Benevolent authoritative

9.2 The contingency view of management focuses attention on

A the relationship between technical and social variables within the system.
B the psychological and social needs of people at work.
C the large number of variables, or situational factors, which influence organisational design and performance.
D the formal structure, technical requirements of the organisation and general set of principles.

9.3 Blake and Mouton designed a managerial grid on which the style of managers can be plotted. Which of the following is NOT a management style they described?

A Team style
B Action-centered style
C Country club style
D Impoverished centre

9.4 Which one of the following is incorrect?

A Authority is a form of power
B Responsibility is the power given to someone by virtue of the position in the organisation
C Managers should be held accountable for the responsibility they are given
D Leadership theory is relevant to organisational management

9.5 Which of the following writers suggested a view of leadership that the style of management that will be most effective in a given situation will depend on the circumstances of that situation (the contingency approach)?

A Hertzberg
B Blake and Mouton
C Adair
D Likert

9.6 Which of the following is NOT one of Weber's eight characteristics of a bureaucracy?

A Specialisation
B Career officials
C Rules
D Scientific selection and development of the worker

☑ Knowledge test – Answers

9.1 C

The wording of the question is almost a definition of the participative style. The other styles are

1. *Exploitative authoritative* – manager makes decision and enforces it
2. *Benevolent authoritative* – manager makes decision and sells it
3. *Consultative* – manager asks for suggestions on what he should decide.

Introduction to Management Theory Leadership

9.2 **C**

A is the socio-technical approach. **B** is the human relations approach.

D refers to the classical approach. The contingency approach suggests that the effectiveness of these approaches vary according to the particular circumstances of the situation.

9.3 **B**

B is the management style described by John Adair. The others together with task-orientated style and the middle of the road are described by Blake and Mouton.

9.4 **B**

This is one element of authority. Responsibility gives someone the charge over or control over something. The person to whom responsibility has been assigned is the person who is in control of ensuring the task is completed even if they delegate the completion of the task to someone else.

9.5 **C**

9.6 **D**

The Management of Groups

The Management of Groups 10

🔑 Behaviour in work groups

A group is

"any collection of people who perceive themselves to be a group" (Handy 1993).

A group has a sense of identity where individuals conform to common norms and goals.

Individuals join groups in order to satisfy some important need (e.g. to feel safe, for friendship, to have a sense of belonging or a sense of purpose). These types of group membership are likely to be voluntary and informal.

Organisations also use groups to perform a variety of important tasks.

Informal groups

- objectives set by the group itself
- often temporary and changes when staff join or leave
- fluid organisations based on norms and roles allocated by group itself
- self-selecting membership
- main aim is the survival of the group and the welfare of its members.

Formal

- objectives mainly set by superior management
- tends to be permanent
- organised according to established structure and procedures
- membership decided by management
- main function is the realisation of organisations' aims.

Teams

A team is a small number of people with complementary skills who are committed to a common purpose, performance goals and approach.

Formation of groups

Tuckman

Tuckman suggested workgroups (together with any other group) pass through four stages of development:

1. *Forming* – making a personal impression, getting to know the others, individuals may possibly drop out at this stage
2. *Storming* – bargaining over goals, resulting in conflict
3. *Norming* – developing agreed ways of working to achieve goals
4. *Performing* – groups now begin to function smoothly and achieve its purpose.

Belbin

Belbin made a long study of the mix of characteristics in a team. He concluded that a team composed of the brightest did not turn out to be the best (The Apollo Syndrome). An effective management team needs to have eight different roles (to which he later added another role):

1. *Chairman* – presides over the team and co-ordinates its efforts
2. *Shaper* – the task leader
3. *Plant* – the source of original ideas and proposals
4. *Monitor evaluator* – dissects ideas and sees the flaws in arguments
5. *Resource investigator* – brings new contacts, ideas and developments to the group
6. *Company worker* – the practical organiser
7. *Team worker* – holds the team together by being supportive
8. *Finisher* – checks detail, worries about schedules and ensures that tasks are finished.

Later Belbin added:

- *Expert* – technical person, if needed, to solve technical problems.

Roles within the team

Ensuring a successful mix of roles within a team is vital but seldom achieved. This is due to

- lack of understanding
- lack of time
- people not available
- misunderstanding of task requirements.

Communication

The role of communication in organisations

- Providing information for planning and control
- Providing information about the organisation to the outside world
- Swapping of ideas and knowledge within the organisation
- Clarification of information
- Informing subordinates
- Developing and maintaining interpersonal relations

- Insurance of links in the value chain
- Resolution of conflict by negotiation.

Communication methods – oral and written

Effective and regular personal communications are vital to ensure project progression and to identify problems quickly.

Oral communication can take many forms:

- face-to-face meetings
- telephone conversations
- videoconferencing.

Written communication is normally achieved by internal memos and e-mails to team members, external letters and regular project reports to customers.

Communication methods – meetings

Meetings are an effective communication method for the project manager, the team members and the customers. In order to ensure that meetings are effective then the following needs to be carried out:

- the purpose of the meeting
- establish who needs to attend
- determine the agenda in advance and distribute to those attending
- make suitable arrangements for the location and time in advance
- facilitate discussion
- manage the plan of action
- summarise
- publish results/minutes.

Roles of team members within meetings

In order for a group to be effective a number of roles need to be established:

- *Facilitator* – He or she should take responsibility for setting the agenda for discussion and ensuring that the meeting achieves its objectives.
- *Chairperson* – His or her main responsibility is to ensure that the agenda for the meeting is followed and that all the members have the ability to participate equally and that all views are listened to.
- *Secretary* – His or her responsibility is to take minutes of the meeting and provide a hard/electronic copy of these minutes to the team member after the meeting.
- *Protagonist/Antagonist* – Any positive supporter/negative detractor of the issues under discussion.

Negotiation

Organisations must negotiate both with outside organisations as well as allowing negotiations to take place with internal stakeholders.

Characteristics of negotiations

- Conflict of interest between two or more parties.
- Either no established set of rules for resolving the conflict, or the parties prefer to work outside of an established set of rules to establish a solution.
- The parties prefer to search for an agreement rather than to openly fight, to have one side capitulate to break off contact permanently or to take their dispute to a higher authority.

Stages of negotiations

- *Preparation* – knowing the background to the problem
- *Opening phase* – both sides presenting their starting points
- *Bargaining phase* – the aim is to narrow the gap between the initial positions
- *Closing phase* – agreement is reached.

Motivating group members

In order to get the most from any group or team, the individuals must be motivated so that they work hard, and in the direction of the group's aims. Practically this will mean:

- Selecting group members who show enthusiasm and alignment with other group members and the group's goals
- Ensuring there is a clear leader who sets a clear direction, uses a democratic management style to get the group's participation and deals with conflicts in the group
- Giving the group as a whole responsibility for their achievements, with related rewards
- Giving individuals responsibility for parts of the group's activities, with related rewards
- Creating competition with similar groups
- Avoiding hygiene factors (Hertzberg) such as poor working conditions, lack of supervision, bureaucracy and internal conflicts.

Mentoring

A mentor is someone who advises and supports another individual (the mentee) to facilitate both their current work and the individual's development. Often mentors are experienced member of staff who can use their experience to support and guide their mentee.

. Benefits of mentoring

- improved motivation among employees
- lower levels of staff turnover
- faster career progress
- fewer and more quickly resolved disputes.

The steps in the mentoring process are:

- *Building the relationship* – getting to know the mentees and building trust between them and the mentor.
- *Negotiating agreements* – defining the mentor and mentee's roles, the timing and regularity of meetings, the basis of the relationship they will have, limitations that may exist.

- *Developing the mentee* – providing guidance, support, counselling, coaching, a sounding board, resourcing and using influence to help the individual.
- *Ending the relationship* – evaluate the progress made against each mentee's goals and the effectiveness of the mentoring and agree how the mentees will continue in their development in the future, outside the mentoring relationship.

Knowledge test – Quick questions

10.1 Research on group effectiveness has concluded that the most consistently successful groups:

    A   are those in which all members are innovative.
    B   comprise a range of roles undertaken by various members.
    C   are those in which all members are very intelligent.
    D   compromise a range of roles all undertaken by a few members of the group.

10.2 Tuckman identified four stages in development. In what order do they occur?

    A   Forming, Storming, Norming and Performing
    B   Forming, Norming, Storming and Performing
    C   Norming, Forming, Storming and Performing
    D   Forming, Performing, Norming and Storming

10.3 A company has established a project team to design a new information system. The team has had a few meetings to discuss how they are going to tackle the work, and who should do what, but some early ideas have been unsuccessful. Group members are still putting forward a number of very innovative ideas, but they often disagree strongly with each other. The group members appear to be dividing into two camps, each of which has had an unofficial leader. These two individuals agree about very little and appear to dislike each other.

According to Tuckman, what stage of development has the project team reached?

    A   Forming
    B   Performing
    C   Norming
    D   Storming

10.4 Which one of the following is NOT one of Belbin's roles for an effective team?

    A   Company worker
    B   Plant
    C   Monitor evaluator
    D   Autocrat

10.5 Which one of the following is NOT one of the roles of communication in organisations?

    A   Providing information for planning and control
    B   Swapping of ideas and knowledge within the organisation
    C   The developing and maintaining interpersonal relations
    D   Establishing goals and objectives

10.6 What according to Tuckman is the definition of Norming?

    A   Making a personal impression, getting to know the others, individuals may possibly drop out at this stage

B Bargaining over goals, resulting in conflict
C Developing agreed ways of working to achieve goals
D Groups now begin to function smoothly and achieve its purpose

10.7 "The source of original ideas and proposals" (Belbin) is known as

A Shaper
B Plant
C Resource investigator
D Team worker

10.8 What is the correct order of the stages of negotiation?

A Preparation, Bargaining Phase, Opening Phase, Closing Phase
B Opening Phase, Preparation, Bargaining Phase, Closing Phase
C Preparation, Opening Phase, Bargaining Phase, Closing Phase
D Opening Phase, Bargsaining Phase, Preparation, Closing Phase

10.9 "The person who takes responsibility for setting the agenda for discussion and ensuring that the meeting achieves its objectives" is a description of which role within meetings?

A Facilitator
B Chairperson
C Secretary
D Protagonist

10.10 "Bringing new contacts, ideas and developments to the group" is a description of which of Belbin's roles within a team?

A Shaper
B Plant
C Monitor evaluator
D Resource investigator

10.11 Handy suggested that the effectiveness of a work group depends on a number of "givens" and a number of "intervening factors". Management can influence both givens and intervening factors to affect the outcomes. Which of the following is a "given"?

A Procedures
B Process
C Leadership style
D The group's environment

10.12 Choose from the list below the word(s) that correctly completes the definition:

"A .... holds the team together by being supportive."
(Chairman, Shaper, Plant, Company worker, Team worker)

(2 marks)

10.13 Choose from the list below the word(s) that correctly completes the definition:

"A .... is the practical organiser."
(Chairman, Shaper, Plant, Company worker, Team worker)

(2 marks)

10.14 According to Tuckman what are the four stages that workgroups pass through as they develop?

(2 marks)

10.15 What is a team?

(2 marks)

Knowledge test – Answers

10.1 **B**

This research was carried out by Belbin. He concluded that a team composed of the brightest did not turn out to be the best (The Apollo Syndrome). An effective management team needs to have eight different roles (to which he later added another role).

10.2 **A**

1. *Forming* – making a personal impression, getting to know the others, possibly dropping out
2. *Storming* – bargaining over goals, resulting in conflict
3. *Norming* – developing an agreed way of working to achieve goals
4. *Performing* – groups now begin to function smoothly.

10.3 **D**

This is the storming stage. During this stage conflict can be quite open.

10.4 **D**

According to Belbin effective management team needs to have eight different roles (to which he later added another role): Chairman, Shaper, Plant, Monitor evaluator, Resource investigator, Company worker, Team worker, Finisher, later Belbin added Expert.

10.5 **D**

The role of communication in organisations includes

- Providing information for planning and control
- Providing information about the organisation to the outside world
- Swapping of ideas and knowledge within the organisation
- Clarification of information
- Informing subordinates
- Developing and maintaining interpersonal relations
- Insurance of links in the value chain
- Resolution of conflict by negotiation.

10.6 **C**

10.7 **B**

Belbin described the four roles in the question thus:

1. *Shaper* – the task leader
2. *Plant* – the source of original ideas and proposals

3. *Resource investigator* – brings new contacts, ideas and developments to the group
4. *Team worker* – holds the team together by being supportive.

10.8 **C**

The stages of negotiation are

- *Preparation* – knowing the background to the problem
- *Opening phase* – both sides presenting their starting points
- *Bargaining phase* – the aim is to narrow the gap between the initial positions
- *Closing phase* – agreement is reached.

10.9 **A**

10.10 **D**

10.11 **D**

The "givens" are the members of the group, the tasks of the group and the group's environment.

10.12 "A Team worker holds the team together by being supportive."

10.13 "A Company worker is the practical organiser."

10.14
1. Forming
2. Storming
3. Norming
4. Performing.

10.15 A team is a small number of people with complementary skills who are committed to a common purpose, performance goals and approach.

Control, Conflict and Discipline

Control, Conflict and Discipline 11

Internal control systems

Levels of control

Organisations can be divided into three hierarchical levels: Strategic (senior management), tactical (middle management) and operational. These organisational decision-making levels can also be used to distinguish the organisational control levels.

Strategic control
This is the level of control operating at board level. It will largely consist of the setting of the control environment. It will include

- strategic planning determining the course the organisation will take
- board procedures
- setting and review of organisational structure
- codes of conduct
- policies on such things as: the conduct of business; financial and other performance measures; recruitment, selection, appraisal, discipline and reward of employees; training and development; environmental and ethical issues; and the risk assessment, risk management and internal control systems.

Tactical control
This is control at the middle management level of the organisation. Controls at tactical level include

- tactical planning determining the production requirements and production schedule
- the production budget
- procedures that govern the human resources; environmental and ethical issues; and risk assessment and risk management
- monitoring achievement of, and compliance with, plans and policies set that relate to the production department.

Operational control

This occurs at the lower levels of the organisation. Operational controls are designed to control structured and repetitive activities according to preset rules. For example, a computerised stock control system, where stock levels per component, reorder levels and reorder quantities are calculated and operated according to predetermined and precise rules.

Managing individuals

As an element of operational control, individuals must be controls. This ensures that each individual is working hard and effectively and avoids detrimental or poor performance. Methods which can be used to control individual behaviour include:

- Employment contracts – Which set out clearly the basis on which the individual will work, and the terms and conditions of employment.
- Job descriptions – These set out an individual's specific roles and responsibilities, help to clarify what they need to do, what they have responsibility for and the level of expected performance in each of these areas.
- Performance appraisals – Reviewing performance against job descriptions and targets provides feedback for the individual on what they are doing well and not so well so helping their development in the future. By aligning achievement of objectives with rewards such as promotion or bonuses, companies ensure staff remain motivated towards the organisation's goals.
- Supervision – This ensure that staff are monitored, to make sure they are abiding by rules and procedures, and also acts as a means of providing support and guidance to improve an individual's work.

Legal issues

Health and safety

Safety, health and the environment
The Health and Safety at Work Act (1975) requires every organisation employing five or more persons to prepare a written statement.

Advisory, Conciliation and Arbitration Service (ACAS) identifies five key areas of *employer responsibility* as specified in the Act:

1. provision and maintenance of safe and risk-free plant and systems of work
2. ensuring the safe use, handling, storage and transport of articles and substances
3. provision of information, training, instruction and supervision
4. maintenance of a safe workplace and the provision of means of entry and exit
5. provision of a safe working environment and adequate facilities (e.g. heating, lighting and toilets).

Employees also have a duty under the act to

- take a reasonable care of themselves or others who may be affected by their acts and omissions
- keep their own working areas tidy and safe
- avoid creating hazards

- draw to management's attention potential problems
- co-operate with their employer so far as is necessary to ensure that the employer can perform their legal duties.

Health and safety training
Health and safety training is the only form of training required by statute.

Categories of health and safety training include

- *Induction for new staff* – All new staff must receive training which ensures their safety both in normal working conditions and in emergency.
- *Monitoring the safety* – There is a legal requirement to notify the authorities of any incident at work resulting in death or a major injury or more than three days of work.
- *Prevention* – To avoid accidents happening.

Working time Directive
The Working Time Directive is an EU law limiting of the maximum length of a working week to 48 hours in 7 days, and a minimum rest period of 11 hours in each 24 hours. In the UK, employees can opt out of this requirement.

Diversity and equal opportunities

In the UK, specific anti-discriminatory employment Acts include the following:

- disabled persons
- equal pay act
- race relations
- fair employment
- gender
- disability
- age.

Diversity is the process of encouraging the employment of people from a wide range of backgrounds, ages, beliefs, religions and so on. This benefits the organisation through providing a wider range of skills and knowledge alongside a potentially more tolerant approach.

Maternity/Paternity leave
In the UK statutory maternity leave is for 52 weeks. Employees may be entitled to receive Statutory Maternity Pay for up to 39 weeks of the leave, the amount being set out by legislation. Father can take up to 2 weeks of paid paternity leave, the exact amount and time they are entitled to does vary depending on the terms of their employment. Often employers will have their own schemes which may be more generous than the statutory minimum.

Fair treatment
Fairness can be thought of in two ways – the moral case (the right thing to do – see the ethics section) and the business case (for the best interests of the business, so fair to shareholders). Directors must strike a balance between all the stakeholder needs, while also recognising that employees need to feel they are treated fairly and equally in order to maintain motivation.

Conflict in organisations

Symptoms

- problems, however, trivial being passed up the hierarchy
- hostility and jealousy between groups
- poor communications up and down the hierarchy
- widespread frustration and dissatisfaction because of the difficulty getting even simple tasks done
- problems being constantly polarised.

Sources of conflict

These may be classified as either horizontal or vertical.

Horizontal conflict
This occurs between groups at the same level within the hierarchy. The sources may be:

- *Environment* – increasing uncertainty and speed of change
- *Size* – increasing size means that departments see themselves separate from the rest of the organisation
- *Technology* – interdependence may lead to conflict
- *Goals* – the accomplishment of goals by one department may have a detrimental effect on another department
- *Structure* – departments may be put in competition for resources
- *Operative goal incompatibility*
- *Differentiation* – differences arise between the cognitive and emotional orientations among managers in different functional departments
- *Task interdependence* – as the level of interdependence increases the potential for conflict increases
- *Uncertainty* – as certainty about departmental relationships increases conflict can be expected to increase
- *Reward system* – the reward system governs the degree to which some groups co-operate or conflict with one another.

Vertical conflict
Vertical conflict occurs among groups at different levels in the vertical hierarchy. Many of the same concepts apply to their tickle conflict but the groups and issues may be different.

Conflict handling strategies

- *Avoidance* – one or more parties in conflict may seek to avoid, suppress or to ignore the conflict
- *Accommodation* – this involves one party putting the other's interests before their own
- *Compromise* – each party gives up something
- *Competition* – this is a state where both parties do not co-operate
- *Collaboration* – this is likely to be the optimum solution. Differences are confronted and jointly resolved, novel solutions are sought and a win-win outcome is achieved.

- *Arbitration* – This is where the parties in dispute agree to abide by the decision of an independent person (the arbiter)
- *Conciliation* – this is where an independent person (the conciliator) meets with the parties separately in an attempt to resolve their differences.
- *Industrial tribunals* – These are independent panels who hear and make legally-binding rulings in relation to employment law disputes.

Discipline

Disciplinary procedures

Many large organisations will have a handbook outlining the steps which formal disciplinary processes must pass through. These are typically endorsed by the trade union. Once established they are legally binding;

- interview in presence of a representative
- written account of meeting
- second interview in presence of representative with written warning of dismissal
- dismissal.

Alternatives to dismissal

- reprimand
- job design
- incentive
- training
- transfer
- support
- release.

Disciplinary sanctions

Sanctions should be:

- Immediate – very difficult if ACAS procedures are followed!
- Consistent
- Impersonal
- Expected – for example, in induction training.

ACAS code of practice

In the UK, most organisational discipline is covered by the ACAS Code of Practice. This specifies the requirements of good disciplinary procedures (e.g. they should be in writing; they should be non-discriminatory) and lays down how disciplinary incidents should be dealt with:

- Thoroughly investigated and a written record made
- First warning – oral or written
- Final written warning – warns of punitive action and explains appeal procedure.

Formal warnings have a limited period of validity (e.g. 12 months).

Knowledge test – Quick questions

11.1 Starting at the top of the organisation an organisation may be divided into three levels. What are they?

   A   Strategic, Tactical, Operational
   B   Strategic, Operational, Tactical
   C   Tactical, Strategic, Operational
   D   Operational, Tactical, Strategic

11.2 Strategic planning determining the course the organisation should take, board procedures, setting and review of organisational structure are all examples of what type of control?

   A   Strategic
   B   Tactical
   C   Operational
   D   Socio-technical

11.3 Procedures that govern the human resources; environmental and ethical issues; and risk assessment and risk management is an example of what type of control?

   A   Strategic
   B   Tactical
   C   Operational
   D   Socio-technical

11.4 A computerised stock control system, where stock levels per component, reorder levels and reorder quantities are calculated and operated according to predetermined and precise rules is an example of what type of control?

   A   Strategic
   B   Tactical
   C   Operational
   D   Socio-technical

11.5 Which of the following is NOT identified by ACAS as a key area of employer responsibility as specified in The Health and Safety at Work Act?

   A   Provision and maintenance of safe and risk-free plant and systems of work
   B   Provision of information, training, instruction and supervision
   C   Provision of adequate leave for parental commitments for parents of children born after 2 May 2004
   D   Maintenance of a safe workplace and the provision of means of entry and exit

11.6 Employees have a duty under The Health and Safety at Work Act to do which of the following?

   A   Attend training courses on Health and Safety
   B   Ensure that they regularly update their technical knowledge
   C   Keep their own working areas tidy and safe
   D   Draw colleagues attention to potential hazards

11.7 In the UK specific anti-discriminatory employment Acts do not include which of the following?

   A Disability
   B Age
   C Race
   D Sex

11.8. In the UK, ACAS provides information and services for organisations. What does ACAS stand for?

   A Advisory Conciliation and Arbitration Service
   B Autonomous Counselling and Advice Service
   C Advice Counselling and Arbitration Service
   D Autonomous Conciliation and Advice Service

11.9 There are a number of initial management responses to handling conflict, but not all are necessarily effective. Which response to handling conflict has the problem of creating lingering resentment?

   A Compromise
   B Denial
   C Dominance
   D Suppression

11.10 ACAS identifies five key areas of employer responsibility. Which is NOT one of them?

   A Provision and maintenance of safe and risk-free plant and systems of work
   B Provision of information, training, instruction and supervision
   C Maintenance of safe workplace
   D Provide specific anti-discriminatory employment

11.11 ACAS code of practice states that in disciplinary procedures a formal warning has a limited period of validity. How long is this term?

   A 6 months
   B 12 months
   C 18 months
   D 24 months

11.12 How long is the validity period of a formal warning under ACAS code of practice?
   (2 marks)

11.13 Identify five conflict handling strategies. **(3 marks)**

11.14 Explain the difference between horizontal and vertical conflict. **(2 marks)**

11.15 List 3 benefits of Health and safety training. **(3 marks)**

11.16 Stress at work is one element of health and safety. However, it is not always bad. Which of the following causes of stress might be deemed positive for the organisation?

   - Family problems
   - Poor time management
   - Lack of skills
   - Unsafe machinery

- Computer problems
- Tough but achievable targets
- Deadlines set to achieve customer needs. **(2 marks)**

☑ Knowledge test – Answers

11.1 **A**

11.2 **A**

Strategic control is the level of control operating at board level.

11.3 **B**

Tactical control is control at the middle management level of the organisation.

11.4 **C**

Organisational controls occur at the lower levels of the organisation.

11.5 **D**

ACAS identifies five key areas of *employer responsibility* as specified in the Act:

1. provision and maintenance of safe and risk-free plant and systems of work
2. ensuring the safe use, handling, storage and transport of articles and substances
3. provision of information, training, instruction and supervision
4. maintenance of a safe workplace and the provision of means of entry and exit
5. provision of a safe working environment and adequate facilities (e.g. heating, lighting and toilets).

11.6 **C**

Employees also have a duty under the act to

- take a reasonable care of themselves or others who may be affected by their acts and omissions
- keep their own working areas tidy and safe
- avoid creating hazards
- draw to management's attention potential problems
- co-operate with their employer so far as is necessary to ensure that the employer can perform their legal duties.

11.7 **B**

In the UK, specific anti-discriminatory employment Acts include the following:

- disabled persons
- equal pay act
- race relations
- fair employment
- sex
- disability.

Only a few discriminatory practices are covered by legislation. Further antidiscrimination legislation in terms of age, sexual orientation and religion or belief is proposed.

11.8   A

11.9   C

Dominances the application of power and authority and will build up/lingering resentment.

11.10 D

The other two of the five key areas are ensuring the safe use, handling, storage and transport of articles and substances and provision of a safe working environment and adequate facilities.

11.11 B

11.12 12 months

11.13 Avoidance, Accommodation, Compromise, Competition, Collaboration.

11.14 Horizontal conflict occurs between groups or individuals at the same level within the hierarchy, whereas vertical conflict occurs between different levels within the organisation's hierarchy.

11.15
1. Preventing accidents
2. Fewer sick days
3. More content staff, knowing they are working in a safe environment.

11.16
- Tough but achievable targets
- Deadlines set to achieve customer needs.

12

Question Bank

Question Bank

12

Questions 1–5 Strategic management

Question 1 – Stakeholders

A school operated by a local administrative authority provides educational opportunities for teenage pupils within an area in a city. The school has achieved varying levels of success in public examinations and, in terms of examination results, is performing neither better nor worse than other comparable schools serving the city. Its teaching and administrative staff are conscientious and committed to providing quality education to the pupils. The head teacher is required to improve the school's success in respect of examination performance, but the local administrative authority is unable to provide any resources beyond those which are already available.

The head teacher works within the following parameters:

- there is a maximum number of pupils that the school can admit each year
- the budgets for the school's teaching activities are allocated in accordance with the subjects which are taught
- the pupils admitted to the school study some core subjects and they may also choose to study some subjects from a range of options, which can be extended or reduced.

Requirement

Identify the stakeholder groups that the school is seeking to serve within its "customer" portfolio and briefly outline their requirements.

(10 marks)

Question 2 – Bryher

The Bryher Company (Bryher) consists of automobile engine, marine engine and aerospace engine businesses. It has built its global reputation for engine design and quality on its engineering capability. Though the marine engine business has not been performing well for some time, Bryher has dominated the supply of engines for the luxury end of the automobile market for years. Unfortunately for Bryher, however, the market in luxury automobiles is changing. Exchange rate movements and increased production costs have made Bryher less competitive and its rivals are rapidly catching up in terms of engine quality and design. As a result, the latest annual report shows turnover down, margins reduced and the company barely breaking even.

You have just attended a strategy meeting at Bryher in which:

- Manager A argued that the automobile engine business strategy was wrong
- Manager B claimed that the major problem had been the failure to properly implement functional strategies.

Requirement

For the benefit of a junior manager explain:

The differences between corporate level strategy, business level strategy and functional level strategy for Bryher.

(10 marks)

Question 3 – V Inc

Mike is the Chief Executive Officer (CEO) of V Inc, a company that makes and distributes alcoholic drinks. In recent years much of the company's growth has been through the introduction and heavy promotion of "Alco pops". Alco pops are sweet alcoholic drinks aimed specifically at the younger drinker. He has traditional views about the purpose of business in general and his own organisation in particular. Though he is frequently pressured by a variety of groups and organisations that think he should run his organisation differently, he sticks firmly to the view that the overriding purpose of business is to make money for the shareholders. His son, Harvey, who is being coached to take over the CEO role, takes a very different perspective. In his view, V Inc has a responsibility to a wide range of stakeholders.

Requirements

Explain how

(a) Mike would justify his view that the overriding purpose of the business is to make money for the shareholders
(b) Harvey would justify his view that V Inc has a responsibility to a wide range of stakeholders.

(10 marks)

Question 4 – The rational model of strategic planning

The rational model of strategic management is a logical and comprehensive approach. It attempts to consider all relevant information and options. However, it is sometimes argued that the rational model has become less relevant in an environment that is increasingly complex and changing at an ever increasing rate.

Requirement

Describe the advantages and disadvantages of using the rational planning approach to strategy formulation for an organisation.

(10 marks)

Question 5 – V plc

V plc operates in the leisure and entertainment industry. It has a range of different ventures worldwide including fitness centres, casinos, cinemas and sports bars, each of which operates as a separate business.

Requirement

Distinguish between the different levels at which strategy should exist in V plc.

(10 marks)

Question 6 – T

T is the owner manager of a small business that designs and produces high quality garden furniture. The business started out as a hobby using T's creative design and carpentry talents, and he has been surprised by his success. Over the last year the business has experienced unplanned growth and by chance T has just won a contract to supply a local chain of DIY stores. The local Chamber of Commerce has recently sent him an invitation to attend a number of seminars entitled "Formal Strategic Planning for Small Businesses". However, T is doubtful that the content of the seminars will be of any relevance to him and feels he cannot afford time away from his business. His view is that it is best to let the strategies and developments for his business emerge.

Requirement

Explain the reasons why T is right to be doubtful about the relevance of formal strategic planning for his business.

(10 marks)

Question 7 – S Company

T is the CEO of S Company, a manufacturer of hair and body care products. Over the years the company has been market leader in its field, achieved through being at the forefront of product innovation. S Company has invested heavily in research and development, which has enabled it to be the first in the market to introduce new variants of the product range. However, this has meant that the cost of operations has spiralled leading to an increase in the price of the company's products.

Up until last year, the company had been very successful in increasing its market share. However, the most recent key performance indicators show that sales are down. It would seem that supermarket 'own brand products' are stealing market share, and T is worried about the future ability of the company to meet its objectives for continued growth. T has decided to undertake a strategic review, the first stage of which will involve conducting a corporate appraisal.

Requirement

Explain what would be involved in undertaking a corporate appraisal, demonstrating how the information could be used to help T in his review.

(10 marks)

Questions 8–10 Project management

ABC Ltd is a medium-sized family-owned company, located in the northern region of a country in the European Community. It manufactures a range of high-quality electrical household goods as well as buying in completed products for resale from a number of suppliers. It sells its products through a variety of outlets, such as mail order catalogue companies, large stores, small retail outlets, and directly to household customers.

The company's computer system was installed 10 years ago, and the directors accept that it needs to be updated. They have many different systems which are not consistent in terms of the information they hold about stock, customers, sales and purchase information, as each department is responsible for only its part of the system. For example, the accounting department keeps a regularly updated file on customers and orders placed, but this data is held separately from the data maintained by the sales department on customers.

The system has proved adequate in the past for areas such as payroll, financial accounting and sales order invoicing, but does not meet the changing information requirements for management decision-making in a competitive market. For example, information relating to stock levels is available to sales staff online, but is often out of date as the master-files are only updated on a weekly basis. Technical faults and breakdowns mean that the system is often unavailable and customers are asked to try again later. Managers at all levels of the company feel that the current system does not meet their information requirements.

The directors, who wish to expand the company both within the region and the whole country, have accepted these recommendations. They are now looking to appoint a temporary Project Manager, to lead a small team responsible for the new systems development project. The directors of ABC Ltd consider that the appointed Project Manager will be required only for a secondment period of approximately 12 months, while the systems development and installation are taking place. After the successful completion of the project, the appointee will return to his or her original position; however, the directors consider this to be an opportunity for a member of staff to gain excellent organisational, management and systems experience.

Question 8
Identify and describe the responsibilities of the Project Manager within ABC Ltd.

(10 marks)

Question 9
Identify and describe the skills that a Project Manager would require to successfully implement a major project involving the design and installation of the new computer system within ABC Ltd.

(10 marks)

Question 10
Describe the importance of objective setting in the success of the project at ABC Ltd and the qualities which would be found in a set of good quality objectives.

(10 marks)

Question 11 (May 2008 Exam)
P is the project manager responsible for managing the relocation of H Company's head office to new premises. He thought all was going well with the project and is very surprised when he learns that various project stakeholders are complaining about his poor communication skills.

Some of the complaints made relate to the complex messages he sends and his use of very technical language associated with the project. Whilst he feels he is keeping the project team members up to date, they feel they are overloaded with e-mails covering lots of different issues, not all of which are relevant to them.

Requirement
Explain to P what he could do to ensure that his communications with stakeholders about the relocation project are more effective.

(10 marks)

Question 12 (May 2008)
S has been working on a major IT project for his client, X Hotel chain. The project brief was to design and implement a customer reservation system, which would enable customers

to book online for rooms at any of X's hotels worldwide. When commissioning the project, the hotel chain required that the new system should be ready to coincide with the launch of its new flagship hotel opening in six months' time.

The project is now in the final stage of its lifecycle and the customer reservation system is ready to "go live". S is from an IT background and this is his first time in the role of project manager. He is finding the whole process of finishing off the final details of the project tedious and is keen to get started with the next project that he is due to manage.

Requirement
Explain to S why project completion is an important activity and explain what is involved during this stage of the project management lifecycle.

(10 marks)

Question 13 (May 2007)

A number of volunteers were so moved by news coverage reporting on the difficulties facing earthquake victims in F country that they organised a sponsored walk to raise funds for the appeal. Two of the volunteers visited some of the worst hit areas and this prompted them to set up their own charity. Their first major project is to rebuild and provide equipment for a school in one of the villages that has been devastated by the disaster. They hope to have the school up and running in twelve months' time. A number of people have been enlisted to help with the project, including some local businesses as well as family and friends. The volunteers realise this will be a more complex project than organising a sponsored walk and therefore will require a much more professional approach to ensure that they achieve their objectives. They have limited experience of managing projects and are trying to determine the purpose of the different phases and activities. P, one of the volunteers, has been given the task of finding out about the first stage, initiating the project, and specifically, how to put together a project initiation document.

Requirement

To help P, describe what is involved in the initiation stage of a project and explain what should be included in the project initiation document for the school project.

Questions 14–19 Management of relationships

Question 14 – Disciplinary procedures

NYO.com was established in February 2000. Since then, the company, which provides online financial advice, has experienced rapid growth and the management has not really had the time to get all management systems and procedures into place.

The company has asked you to look at the way in which the company deals with its disciplinary problems and procedures. The Chief Executive Officer (CEO) has asked you to do two things.

Requirement
Recommend guidelines for drawing up a disciplinary procedure.

(10 marks)

Question 15 – Tauranga

Sean qualified as a doctor before deciding to set up a firm (Tauranga Ltd) carrying out research and development for pharmaceutical firms. The firm has grown to employ around

30 people and has a turnover of £15m. Tauranga specialises in the final stages of pharmaceutical research (so called P3 research).

Sean employs a personal assistant. The assistant has been with the organisation since the commencement of trading. Unfortunately in recent months, Sean has become increasingly unhappy with the performance and attitude of his assistant.

Requirements
(a) What are the alternatives to dismissal for an under performing subordinate?

(5 marks)

(b) If Sean decides to dismiss the assistant what would be the procedures that you recommend?

(5 marks)

Question 16 – Take me to your leader
It has been observed that different styles of leadership are required at different stages of an organisation's development.

Requirement
Define "leadership style" and illustrate your answer with reference to any ONE well-known classification of leadership styles.

(10 marks)

Question 17 – The Northern College
The Northern College is a college in the UK. The majority of college's funding comes from central government funding. Because of its failure to serve a sufficient number of students and to meet quality thresholds, the college has had its funding cut for three consecutive years.

The funding cuts are putting pressure on people throughout the organisation. Departments and individuals have been set more demanding targets, and large-scale redundancies have recently been announced.

This has resulted in considerable conflict. The lecturing professionals are convinced that the marketing department is responsible for the troubles of the organisation. This view is not shared by the marketing people. They believe that the poor quality of service offered is the real reason for the decline in demand for services and for the resulting cuts in government funding. The effect of these differences between departments is one of declining co-operation between the lecturers and the personnel in marketing and sales.

Of more immediate concern to senior management, however, is the threat of industrial action by the trades unions determined to protect their members' jobs. Even individuals such as the management accountant are finding themselves in conflict with departmental managers with whom they have previously enjoyed good relations. Requests for information on costs of providing services are being met with hostility and the management accountant's job becomes more difficult day by day.

Requirement
Discuss the potential consequences arising from the conflicts between various departments and groups within the college.

(10 marks)

Question 18 – Disposable BBQs

Castaway BBQ Ltd (Castaway) was established 10 years ago by Gordon and Katy. The company imported disposable and portable barbeques from China. The barbeques were then sold to the public through a range of intermediaries – retailers and wholesalers. Castaway limited itself to sales within its domestic market. In the first few years of operation Castaway was incredibly successful both in terms of market share and profitability.

Three months ago the founders decided that they would expand their operations by entering the market of a nearby country. Gordon and Katy decided that they would employ an entirely new team to run the operation in the new country. Gordon sees himself as a practical organiser and decided to employ people who, in Gordon's words, were happy to "get things sorted quickly and efficiently – with no messing about!"

Although initial orders have been encouraging they are constantly hearing that there are serious issues with regard to the team. The team is constantly arguing and seems to lack direction. Indeed, two of the senior management team are threatening to resign if things don't improve.

Requirements
(a) Explain the four stages that Tuckman suggested workgroups pass through as they develop. At what stage is the new team?

(5 marks)

(b) What are the different roles that Belbin suggested are needed for an effective management team?

(5 marks)

This has resulted in considerable conflict. The lecturing professionals are convinced that the marketing department is responsible for the troubles of the organisation. This view is not shared by the marketing people. They believe that the poor quality of service offered is the real reason for the decline in demand for services and for the resulting cuts in government funding. The effect of these differences between departments is one of declining co-operation between the lecturers and the personnel in marketing and sales.

Of more immediate concern to senior management, however, is the threat of industrial action by the trades unions determined to protect their members' jobs. Even individuals such as the management accountant are finding themselves in conflict with departmental managers with whom they have previously enjoyed good relations. Requests for information on costs of providing services are being met with hostility and the management accountant's job becomes more difficult day by day.

Requirement
Discuss the potential consequences arising from the conflicts between various departments and groups within the college

(10 marks)

Question 19 (May 2007)

M is Chairman and Managing Director of Y Company which he started 15 years ago, specialising in the manufacture of hospital uniforms. The company has been very successful and, through a series of acquisitions, has diversified into the manufacture of a range of corporate and other uniforms, employing 3,500 people. M is a major force in the company. His management style is very autocratic, and he is unwilling to involve others in decisions about the future strategic direction of the company. Recently, M announced to the Board that he is intending that Y Company becomes listed on the stock exchange.

D, the Finance Director of the company has become increasingly concerned about the decisions being made by M and the fact that he has put pressure on her to participate in some questionable accounting practices. She has had to cover up M's substantial remuneration package, which M has awarded to himself. D is also aware that M has accepted bribes from foreign suppliers and of insider dealing relating to a number of the acquisitions. There is a lack of appropriate control systems and accountability in the company.

D has discussed her concerns with other members of the Board, all of whom work for Y Company, including the Marketing Director, Production Director and HR Director. However, they seem willing to overlook the wrongdoings of M and never challenge the decisions made by him. The opportunity to do so is limited since the Board meets on an irregular and infrequent basis. At the last Board meeting M set out his plans to close the existing factories and move operations to L country where he has been in secret negotiations with representatives of the government. The main objective is to benefit from low cost labour, since the country has very little employment legislation to protect workers and has a poor human rights record.

Requirement
Explain the corporate governance and ethical issues facing Y Company.

(10 marks)

Scenario-based questions

Scenario 1 – Strategic management (Questions 20–22)

Question 20 – Tresco Insurance
Tresco was an old-established insurance company, offering life insurance, pensions, mortgages and related products. It turned itself into a plc six months ago having previously been a mutual company, owned by those taking out insurance policies.

Top management consisted of a Chief Executive Officer (CEO), Sales, Investment and Finance Directors. The Chief Executive and the Directors were appointed by the policy holders. In practice, policy holders never attended the annual meetings, and the Directors reappointed themselves.

The performance of the company was judged by the bonuses provided on insurance policies maturing after 10 years or longer. It depended on the investment and actuarial abilities of the company, rather than on its efficiency.

In the past, all sales have been through company salespersons, paid by commission only. They were chosen for their initiative and interpersonal skills, left to manage on their own and were able to achieve unusually high earnings. They were based in branch offices, each with a manager. Nominally, reporting lines were upwards to the Sales Director, but little information was passed in practice.

In recent years, banks and other financial institutions have entered the insurance market, often with novel tax-saving financial products and innovative sales strategies such as direct telephone selling.

Changes in senior management

When the plc was formed, the CEO became Chairman of the new board of directors and recruited a new Chief Executive from outside the organisation. He in turn recruited a Marketing Director to whom the former Sales Director reports.

Because many customers were sold policies which were not appropriate to their circumstances, the regulations regarding insurance policies and other financial products have been tightened up and revised several times. All policies sold over the last few years will have to be re-examined to meet regulators' requirements. For this purpose a compliance department has been set up.

One of the first proposals of the new Marketing Director was to focus sales on new clients, whose attitude to the organisation was untainted by past errors, rather than on existing clients. The branch managers disagreed with this because of the close relations the salespersons have with the existing clients. The branch managers' attitude was supported by the Finance Director, who feared a loss of revenue.

Salespersons now are carefully trained to complete several pages of questionnaires and to follow standard procedures in dealing with clients. To reduce costs they have been switched to a salaried reward system, and it is hoped that this will also prevent the sale of policies not suitable for the client.

The company is also introducing direct selling by telephone, as a method of reducing costs. The Marketing Director has created two separate divisions – one for personal selling and the other for telephone selling.

Requirements

Organisational culture is the set of values, guiding beliefs and ways of thinking that are shared by members of an organisation.

(a) Identify the cultural features within Tresco.

(12 marks)

(b) Discuss what changes in culture may be required to correspond to the changes made in Tresco.

(13 marks)

Question 21 – The blues

Rummidge Football Club (RFC), a profit-making company with directors and shareholders, has received a takeover bid from one of the satellite-broadcasting corporations. The club is currently assessing whether to accept the bid.

RFC is a multi-million dollar business. Its income consists of gate receipts, fees for TV rights, merchandising, sponsorship, conferencing and catering. The club is very successful; the team's performance on the pitch has made it a very popular club and this success has been reflected in growth in turnover and profits in recent years. The advent of satellite TV has made football a worldwide spectator sport and the club has fans throughout the world.

The success of the club has not, however, prevented it from receiving some criticism. One of the issues causing continuing concern has been the constantly changing replica shirts as worn by the club's football team. Parents of young fans have felt pressurised into spending large sums of money every year or so because the club has changed its shirt style six times in as many years.

Another issue has been the increase in ticket prices over the past few years. These have risen far faster than inflation, and the fan club has made several representations to the board of RFC in protest at these increases.

The income from TV rights is much welcomed by the club, but matches have been rescheduled at short notice to suit satellite stations and their exclusive audiences. It is perhaps not surprising therefore that the bid to take over the club by the satellite-broadcasting corporation has been met with hostility by the fans and others who see the club they have supported and the game they love as being treated like any other profit-making organisation.

(a) Who are the stakeholder groups of the RFC? Describe the particular interest of each stakeholder group in the club.

(12 marks)

(b) Explain which stakeholder groups are likely to exert the most influence on the decision to accept/reject the takeover bid, indicating their power and influence.

(7 marks)

(c) The directors claim that there has been a slow change in policy at the club. Explain the concept of Logical Incrementalism.

(6 marks)

Question 22 – Strategy approaches

Different approaches to strategy formulation were developed throughout the twentieth century. These approaches have included the rational strategy process, emergent strategies and logical incrementalism. The rational strategy approach may be classified as a formal method of strategy formulation. Emergent strategies and logical incrementalism are regarded as informal approaches to strategy formulation.

Compare and contrast the rational strategy approach with emergent strategies and logical incrementalism within the private sector environment.

(25 marks)

Scenario 2 – Project management (Questions 23–25)

Farchester Games

You are a trainee management accountant working for a firm of financial and management consultants (ZX Consultants) who have been contracted to assist in the management and control of a large sporting event due to take place in the region in two years' time.

The World Youth Indoor Games, November 2006

The World Youth Indoor Games is a sporting competition which, every two years, brings together over 5,000 young sportsmen and women from around the world to compete at the highest level in a range of indoor sporting events. The organisation of the Games is a large scale and complex project, involving a diverse range of activities. The strict time constraints set for the project increase the difficulties of managing the other key constraints, namely cost and quality. The next Games are to be held in Farchester, a state capital in the USA, in two years' time, and will last for two weeks.

Project sponsor

The Farchester city government will guarantee to cover the cost of the Games. A significant part of the project will be the provision of new buildings and facilities. A number of the required buildings already exist, and most of the remaining requirements will be constructed as part of a re-development programme being undertaken by Farchester's city government.

Major new works associated with the project include the construction of a 30,000-seat indoor athletics stadium and a world press and media centre.

A further consideration is the upgrade of the current transport network, with major development work required on the local rail system between the main stadium and the city centre, and an airport bus link.

Farchester Games Coordination Committee (FGCC)

The overall management of the project, including the construction of the new facilities and the *refurbishment* of existing facilities, is being co-ordinated by the FGCC. The Committee is made up of local councillors, local businessmen and women, city government officials, sportsmen and women and senior managers from ZX Consultants. In addition to the provision of sporting facilities, transport and accommodation, the scope of the project includes provision of:

- communication facilities
- marketing
- fund raising
- recruitment and training for staff
- organisation of events and ceremonies

These individual project activities are being managed by specialist teams, who are responsible for the delivery of the individual aspects of the project and reporting back to the Committee on a regular basis. Each specialist team is led by a project team manager.

Definition and objectives of the project

There are many stakeholders involved in this project: the paying spectators, the local citizens of Farchester, the state citizens, the sponsors and television companies, the athletes and the location business community. Success will be measured in terms of trouble-free performance of the events, level of customer enthusiasm and satisfaction and sustained economic activities generated in the region. Completion of the project on time is critical; the Games must begin on 2 November 2006. The current date is November 2004 and the FGCC held its first official project meeting on the first day of this month.

Telecommunications and Information Technology

The last three World Youth Indoor Games have attracted a worldwide television audience, and the telecommunications network has to be adequate to cope with the additional television and telephone communications required to facilitate coverage throughout the world. A telecommunications infrastructure, including broadband web transmission and satellite communications, needs to be established to service both national and international demand.

Software requirements

The main software development aspect of the project is the development of the Games communications software in the form of an information database, designed to provide Games information to the general public. This will require development of a dedicated website to give public access to event information. The database will contain information about

- all competitors
- which events they are competing in
- at what time
- where each event is taking place
- the capacity of the building for each event
- the availability of tickets

The database will be designed to allow the general public to monitor the events they are interested in and to allow the Games' co-ordinators to monitor progress of the Games both before and during events. In addition, the public will be able to order tickets from the website for any event and purchase Games merchandise. The website will also contain links to local hotels and restaurant facilities. The whole package of communications software and the telecommunications and IT hardware has been called the "Communications Infrastructure".

Project activities

The project can be broken down into the following areas of work:

Activity	Activity description	Preceding activity	Duration (after completion of preceding activities) (weeks)
A	Obtain financing and sponsorship negotiation	–	22
B	Sporting facilities (refurbishment and new construction)	–	52
C	Analysis of design of communications software	A	14
D	Construct media facilities	B, C	16
E	Program communications system	C	26
F	Install communications software and telecommunications hardware	D, E	6
G	Transport network update and construct athletes' accommodation	–	40
H	Security arrangements and checks (both physical and technological)	G, F	12
I	Public relations/advertising/marketing	F	10
J	Human resources and volunteers (including pre-Games training for volunteers)	I	12
K	Test games, trial events and media systems and contingency	H, J	6
L	Events (including the opening and closing ceremonies)	K	2

Each of the above activities is carried out by individual specialist project teams and is led by a project team manager. It is critical that these events are co-ordinated and planned effectively, as timing is critical to the success of this project. Overall co-ordination of the project is undertaken by the Project Director.

Question 23

(a) What issues need to be addressed in a feasibility study for developing a website for the games?

(13 marks)

(b) Excluding a feasibility study, what are the key activities that the project manager of each of the project team must undertake before the project delivery activities can begin.

(12 marks)

Question 24

(a) Explain what is meant by the cost, time and quality trade-off and what this means for the games.

(7 marks)

(b) Explain how each of these three elements can be effectively controlled for the games project.

(18 marks)

Question 25

For the meeting in December 2004 you have been asked by the FGCC to prepare a report, which includes

(a) an explanation of the importance of undertaking critical path analysis for a project such as the Farchester Games.

(5 marks)

(b) a critical path analysis for the Games clearly identifying:

    (i)   the critical path activities and the critical duration of the project
    (ii) the Earliest Event Time for each activity (EET)
    (iii) the Latest Event Time for each activity (LET).

(16 marks)

(c) calculation of the slack time on activity H and an explanation of how this information may assist decision-making during this project.

(4 marks)

Scenario 3 – Management of relationships (Questions 26–28)

Question 26 – The Coromandel Textile Company

The Coromandel Textile Company (CTC) is in a troubled state. The trade union representing the weavers has just negotiated a pay increase for its members, and this has led to a claim by the mechanics, who maintain the machinery, for a similar percentage pay increase so that the traditional differential with the weavers is maintained. CTC is seeking to resist the mechanics' claim on the grounds that the weavers' extra payment can be justified by increases in productivity, while the maintenance work carried out by the mechanics has not changed. The response of the mechanics has been to threaten industrial action.

The problems for CTC have been made worse by a dispute between the Weaving Department and the Cloth Inspection Department. All members of the Weaving Department, including the weaving shed managers and its supervisors, receive a bonus based on the productivity of the whole department. Employees in the Cloth Inspection Department are paid a fixed salary based on proven competence and experience.

The conflict between the departments developed following the appointment of a new manager in the Cloth Inspection Department. The Works Manager has warned the new manager that the quality of output has to improve if the company is to remain competitive. This has resulted in a general tightening up of the standards enforced in the inspection process so that weaving machines are standing idle more frequently than in the past while faults detected during cloth inspection are investigated. The sight of idle machines has resulted in intense frustration among management and employees in the Weaving Department as every idle machine means a reduction in their bonus payments. The weavers' frustration is now being taken out on the Cloth Inspection Department by adopting a policy of not co-operating.

Requirements
(a) Explain the causes of the horizontal and vertical conflicts within the Coromandel Textile Company.

(10 marks)

(b) Discuss how conflict within the Coromandel Textile Company be dealt with. Explain what factors might influence the likelihood of a successful outcome for the areas of conflict identified.

(15 marks)

Question 27 – Helen Stoakley
Before taking up her position as head of the finance department of the SOFT Corporation, Helen Stoakley had enjoyed a career in the army where she had attained the rank of major. The military style of command had suited her personality. She is by nature an assertive kind of individual, so giving orders is something that comes naturally to her.

The start of her new post of head of finance has not been easy. She has found that her previous style of management has not been well received by her new staff. Her enthusiasm for improving the way things are done in the department is not matched by that of her staff. In fact, if anything an air of resentment seems to exist in the department. More generally, she is finding it difficult to adjust to the whole way of operating in the SOFT Corporation. In her view so much time seems to be spent in meetings and in consultation generally that she wonders how the organisation manages to compete in the market place as successfully as it does.

Requirements
(a) Using an appropriate theory of management style, explain why Helen is experiencing the difficulties described in her new post, and recommend the kind of management style which might be more appropriate.

(12 marks)

(b) A colleague of Helen has noted that retention rates for staff are very poor. Discuss ways in which the organisation can reduce an unacceptable level of staff turnover.

(13 marks)

Question 28 – Max Tools Ltd
Max Tools Ltd is a small machine tooling business based in a Yorkshire town in the UK. They specialise in making tools for large manufacturing companies. This industry does not

experience significant changes. Robert Denney is the managing director of the business and is concerned about the level of productivity of his staff. They are regularly late into work and when they do arrive, they work at what seems to his as a "snail's pace". Lunchtimes are often extended beyond what Robert thinks is necessary.

Much of the work on the production line is repetitive in nature and physically tiring. Many staff argue that they need regular breaks as a result. Staff on the production line are paid just above the minimum wage, since these are low skilled positions.

Robert runs the business using an entrepreneurial structure. He manages all 40 staff with no other hierarchy. He believes that this should encourage staff to take responsibility for their own work and thus be more motivated. He aims to undertake staff reviews annually although the pressures of work rarely allow for this.

One member of the administration team who recently left said that she had become frustrated at the lack of training, and she wanted to go somewhere where she could develop herself. She also commented that the regular disputes between production and administration staff had finally taken their toll.

Requirements
(a) Explain Robert Denney's management style and its suitability for managing Max Tools. If relevant, recommend an alternative style and the structural changes that will be required as a result.

(15 marks)

(b) How could Robert use the ideas of scientific management to improve productivity?

(10 marks)

Question 29 (May 2008)

T works for J Company which designs and manufactures children's toys. She has recently been appointed as the project manager of a project to design a new range of educational toys for children aged 3–6 years. She is currently thinking about the issues that will face her in delivering the objectives of the project. She is confident that she has a good understanding of what needs to happen at the various stages of the project lifecycle and has strong technical skills which will help her in using some of the project management tools and techniques.

T realises that this will not be enough to ensure successful project outcomes and knows that it will be important to have a good project team. However, she is also concerned that people working in teams can sometimes be problematic, particularly since the project team will be made up of people from different parts of the organisation who have not worked together before. The team members will come from finance, marketing, production, IT and sales.

(a) Describe the stages of group formation, as suggested by researchers that T's project team should pass through if it is to become effective in performing the project task.

(10 marks)

(b) Explain the potential problems that could hinder the effectiveness of T's project team and explain how they might be overcome.

(15 marks)
(25 marks)

Question 30 (May 2007)

Over the years, D, an entrepreneur, has had a number of business successes in the retail sector. She is keen to move on to bigger things and has identified an opportunity to develop a Shopping Centre.

Having secured the interest of several potential investors, identified a suitable site, had an architect draw up plans and received planning permission, D is eager that construction work on the Shopping Centre should start as soon as possible. She appointed G, who has an impressive record of managing successful projects, to be project manager. However, D is already interfering in the management of the project and is in conflict with G. She is frustrated by the time G seems to need in the planning phase and is irritated by his insistence on formalising the project management process. D is now putting pressure on G to miss out elements in the first stages of planning the project and to get started on the construction work for the Shopping Centre.

Requirements
(a) Explain the potential problems that the Shopping Centre project could face without good project planning.

(10 marks)

(b) Explain the contribution of different project management tools and techniques that could help G in planning the project.

(15 marks)
(25 marks)

Question 31 – Chocolate Company (Nov 2007)
C Chocolate Company makes and supplies high quality hand made chocolate products. Since the launch of its internet business, it has experienced huge success and is currently enjoying its position as market leader and has built up a strong brand.

The owner of the business attributes much of the success to a combination of factors, including the unique recipes and the skills of staff associated with hand made chocolates and the procurement of high quality cocoa beans. The company's marketing capability and use of IT in developing the company's website has enabled it to track and quickly spot trends in changes to consumer buying patterns. It is clear from the company's research information that to prosper in the industry, constant product innovation is critical in building and maintaining the customer relationship. The flexible approach to new product development allows the company to quickly come up with new chocolate products.

Requirements
(a) Explain the extent to which C Chocolate Company is adopting this strategic approach to gain competitive advantage, making reference to the principles of the Resource Based View.

(13 marks)

(b) Demonstrate how the value chain framework would assist C Chocolate Company in understanding its internal position.

(12 marks)
(25 marks)

Solutions

Solutions

13

Answers to questions 1-5 Strategic management

Question 1 – Stakeholders

Stakeholders are those individuals, or groups of individuals who have an interest in what an organisation does. In the case of the school the following stakeholders, who may also be seen as "customers", may be identified.

- *Students and their parents.* They will demand a good education that leads to success in examinations and eventually their chosen career. In addition they will want to see that the school offers their chosen optional subjects. The school should also be able to offer the students their required combination of subjects.
- *The outside community.* It needs educated and skilled workers. This is both for commercial reasons and also it would be looking for the school to produce individuals who will contribute in some way to community life.
- *Suppliers that deal with the school.* Examples of these may be those helping with the recruitment of staff, stationery suppliers and academic publishers. They will want certainty of supply, certainty of payment and to know that the school can pay them a fair price for their services.
- *The local administrative authority.* This is itself an interested stakeholder as it allocates the funding from the budget for which it is responsible. It needs to ensure that the school is using its resources properly and that they would not be better spent elsewhere (by being allocated to another school for example). It will attempt to ensure that finite resources are used efficiently (maximum output for a given level of input), effectively (producing the right output) and that are resources of a given quality (e.g. staff, cleaning) is bought as cheaply as possible.
- *The Government (local and national).* They too will be concerned with the effective and efficient use of resources. They will also be concerned with the level of exam success. It will also be concerned with issues such as employment rates for the graduating students and the tax and employment opportunities that will be generated. Within the school they will be concerned with social welfare issues such as Health and Safety issues and equal opportunities.
- *Further and higher education colleges.* These will be interested in the students coming out of the college and the level of their achievement for higher education in universities or vocational training centres.
- *Any other interested parties.* The school will scan its environment to look at their needs and objectives. Examples of these may be pressure groups and local residents.

Question 2 – Bryher

Strategies can be developed at three different levels in organisations. These may be seen as follows.

Corporate strategy

This is for the organisation as a whole and considers:

- Which business areas to operate in? What should Bryher sell?
- Which markets to sell to? Who should Bryher sell to?
- Financing the business. How and where should Bryher source its finance?
- Meeting shareholder needs. Deciding how Bryher can meet these needs. It should consider its dividend policy, that is, how much of profits should be paid in dividends and how much retained within the business.
- Organisational structure. What structure should Bryher adopt. Should it be a flat or a tall organisation.

Business strategy

Bryher has a number of different divisions. Each division is likely to have different competitors, customers, suppliers and other stakeholders, and so a division specific strategy is required. Such divisions are called strategic business units (SBUs). Each division will have its own strategy. These business strategies consider

- Products and product features
- Which markets?
- Direct competition and how to be competitive
- Marketing approach
- Business resources (people, buildings, machinery).

Functional/operational strategies

For each function or operational area (e.g. IT, R&D, HR, etc.), a strategy is devised to act as a long-term plan which will support the overall strategy of the business unit. So, for example, the Research and Development department will have a strategy on how it might meet the aims and objectives of the automobile division.

The corporate level strategy, business level strategy and functional level strategy should all be consistent. These strategies should be consistent vertically and horizontally within Bryher as well as consistent over time.

Question 3 – V Inc

(a) Mike could support his view that the purpose of V Inc is to make money for the shareholders to the exclusion other interests, by using the arguments below.

A business is owned by its shareholders. Property rights are fundamental to a free society and an effic economy and should not be infringed without very good reason. Such infringements must be sanctioned by law. If the aim of maximising shareholder value is subordinated to any other goal, the shareholders' assets are being misused.

Even if it is accepted that groups other than shareholders are intimately affected by a company's behaviour, many of those groups' legitimate concerns are satisfied by their contractual relationships with the company. Staff are paid salaries. Suppliers are paid for their supplies. Customers are provided with the products they require and pay for. Taxes are paid to central and local government.

Other groups may feel that they have an interest in what companies do. In the case of a drink's company, which may source its raw material from poorer countries, exploiting cheap labour in the process; which may cause pollution in its manufacturing operations; and which may be accused of marketing dangerous substances without proper controls, there is likely to be a large, vocal, well-organised and powerful body of opinion about its activities. The anti-alcohol lobby will do what it can to hamper V Inc's activities. The correct response to such action is to point out the legal position. It is for government, not pressure groups, to decide what is legal and what is not and the extent to which companies have responsibilities to society at large.

(b) The stakeholder view of organisations' social responsibility is based on the idea that people have inalienable natural rights in addition to any granted by the law as it exists from time to time. Harvey might argue along the lines below:

Large companies, in particular, control so much in the way of resources that their conduct has wider implications for society than just its commercial effects. They also do not bear the total cost of their activities, since many externalities exist. This should be recognised by the companies themselves and they should acknowledge their duty to society.

Corporations' relationship with government through the mechanism of tax is subject to manipulation. Many companies do not pay a fair amount of tax. An acceptance of social responsibility can go some way to compensate for this.

Employees' relationship with their employment is such that they establish greater rights than simply the right to remuneration. They invest a great deal of their lives and personal consequence in their work and deserve to be treated with care and consideration.

Question 4 The rational model of strategic planning

Advantages
The planning approach helps the organisation to take a long view and avoid short-termism while at the same time providing a sensible approach to the uncertainty of the future.

A further advantage is that it provides a clear purpose and direction for the organisation as whole. This is because the starting point for the rational model is the Mission statement of the organisation. Once the mission has been established then the objectives will be established. The organisation's strategy will then be explicitly based around achieving these objectives.

A rational plan will encourage co-ordination of various parts of the organisation, ensuring the integration of operational management decisions into higher strategy, the wider organisational context and longer-term goals.

The process of putting together a plan using the rational approach in itself will be beneficial to the staff involved. They will be both more motivated and have a clearer understanding of the organisation and the environment in which it operates.

Disadvantages
Perhaps the most obvious problem of using the rational model for planning is that it is complex and time consuming. The process involves senior staff and on occasions external consultants. There is, therefore, a considerable cost involved in terms of both financial outlay and time spent.

The formal approach may encourage a spurious sense of control amongst the planners. As the question suggests the environment in which organisations operate is complex and changing at an increasing rate.

The planners might find that they become detached from the organisation. Strategy may then become divorced from operations. Two problems emerge from this. First, the planners may not consider operational implementation issues and secondly staff not involved in the planning process may misunderstand or resist the plans they are required to implement.

A number of writers have suggested that great strategies may not be rational at all but should come from inspiration and entrepreneurial talent. Famously, the head of the Virgin group Richard Branson claims never to have read a business strategy textbook.

Question 5 V plc

Strategy will exist at different levels within V plc, and can be classified in terms of corporate, business and functional. The different levels of strategy can be viewed as a hierarchy whereby activities at the lowest level are guided by and constrained by decisions at the higher levels. In other words the different levels of strategic decisions are interdependent so that one level should be consistent with the strategies at the next level. While the corporate strategic decisions tend to be the concern of senior management, other levels of management in V plc will be responsible for ensuring the successful implementation of strategy.

In order to distinguish between the different levels it is helpful to explore the purpose of each level.

Corporate level strategy in V plc will primarily address the question of what type of business the organisation should be in. It is concerned with its overall purpose and scope. This will involve decisions about the longer term direction of V plc, its activities, matching these to its environment, its resources and values and the expectations of different stakeholders. It is also concerned with how much investment V plc should provide to each of its business units.

Corporate strategy will be encapsulated in V plc's mission and will address decisions such as future acquisitions, mergers, divestments, demergers or closure of its businesses. Also, at corporate level strategic decisions will be made on whether V plc should invest in new businesses, enter new markets or diversify – at the moment the various businesses are all related to the leisure and entertainment industry. This level of strategy provides a framework of goals and objectives that inform the lower levels of strategy for V plc.

Business level strategy should be formulated within the broad framework of the objectives determined by the corporate strategy of V plc. This usually occurs within a strategic business unit (SBU) which is a section within a larger organisation responsible for planning and developing its own products and services. Each SBU will determine its own strategy for its particular market. In V plc the fitness centres, casinos, cinemas and sports bars are all SBUs. Each SBU will make strategic decisions about its range of products/services, how to meet the needs of customers, and how to gain competitive advantage over its competitors. For instance this will involve decisions on which products/services should be developed and how each SBU should segment its markets/s.

Functional strategies, whilst of strategic importance, will be made at operational level in V plc. They are concerned with ensuring that the various functions of the organisation such as production, marketing, finance, human resources, etc., contribute to the achievement of corporate goals and objectives. It is the level at which strategy is implemented in detail. To accomplish this, resources need to be available.

The activities of functional departments of V plc need to reflect the overall strategic direction, otherwise it can counter the direction of the overall organisation. Hence, there needs to be both top-down and bottom-up communications and co-ordination of activities.

Question 6 – T

The formal approach to strategic planning usually results in a consciously thought out or deliberately intended strategy. It assumes that strategy making is a rational process with strategies based on careful analysis of the opportunities and threats posed by the external environment, and consideration of the organisation's strengths and weaknesses, relative to other players in the industry.

Whilst there can be benefits to adopting such an approach, the formal process may not be suitable for a small business such as T's for the following reasons.

- A formal approach can be very expensive, time consuming and complicated for small businesses. T is right to be concerned about the opportunity cost, not only in terms of attending the seminars, but also in terms of spending time on planning which could take him away from the main operations of his business.
- Formal planning may also be considered too static and a process that tends to be infrequent. In a rapidly changing environment it could be argued that the outcomes on which formally planned strategies are based often become quickly outdated, with the result that the intended strategy fails.
- T may be worried that such a process will just end up as a bureaucratic process with systems and targets unhelpful to a small business. The formal approach could get in the way of T's interest and creative talent, since it could be conceived as a rigid approach bound up in processes, undermining T's core competencies.
- One of the aims of formal strategic planning is to achieve goal congruence between different business areas and stakeholders. However in the case of a small business the goals are likely to be inseparable from the goals of T as the owner manager. In a small business, such as that run by T, it could be argued that the formal approach is not appropriate because the success is more dependent on the ideas of T. It is unlikely that T will have the economic rationality in his approach to running the business which is more often associated with businesses governed by external shareholders.
- Even if new options are identified from formal planning T is likely to consider narrow product/market choices because his business is essentially based on his own specific knowledge and skills arising from his hobby. Despite winning the contract from the DIY stores, as a small business it is doubtful that T will have the resources to invest in new strategic ventures and may be unwilling to share or delegate control to others. Indeed T may not have aspirations for growth.
- T says that he prefers to let his strategy emerge. This approach arises from ad-hoc, unanticipated or uncontrollable circumstances. It is often referred to as developing from patterns of behaviour in response to unexpected events. In the case of the scenario T won by chance the order from the local chain of DIY stores. This was not a consciously thought out nor a deliberately intended strategy.

    Whilst there are many valid reasons why T might not see the seminars of any benefit to him, some of the strategic planning frameworks/models might be helpful in making future decisions about the business. For example, it would be sensible for T to monitor the environment and conduct an informal analysis of his strengths, weaknesses, opportunities and threats to help him to stay ahead of the game.

Question 7 – S Company

The outcomes from a corporate appraisal will help T assess the current position of the hair and body care company and its ability to achieve its objectives in the future. This involves assessing the key influences from the external business environment and the internal strategic capability of S Company that will impact on strategy development. It can be used as the basis against which to judge strategic choices.

The internal review of current performance, commonly referred to as a position audit, is undertaken to assess the strategic capability of the company. This would involve auditing the company's resources, products, markets, brands, operations such as research and development, production and distribution and internal structures. A framework that could be used in this process is the value chain. Undertaking value chain analysis can help to identify strengths or core competences, such as the ability to constantly innovate and sources of weaknesses, for instance which of S Company's operations are particularly costly. The outcomes from the analysis will help T understand where value is being added or destroyed and to identify the company's strengths and weaknesses.

Strengths are areas of the company that should be exploited by suitable strategies. In the case of the hair and body care company, strength might be the research and development capability to constantly innovate. Any areas of the company that create weaknesses will need strategies to improve them, for example this might be the cost and efficiency of operations.

Information to feed into the corporate appraisal will also be needed on the external business environment, in terms of the key trends and how these are likely to change in the future. This is often conducted using the PESTEL framework which helps to identify influences that might impact on the strategic development of the company under the headings: political, economic, social, technological, environmental and legal. In addition, competitor analysis will also need to be conducted to assess the nature of the competition. T could use Porter's five forces model to assess the competitive forces that are influencing the nature of competition in the hair and body care industry.

The external appraisal helps to identify opportunities that can be exploited by the company's strengths and also to anticipate possible environmental threats against which it must develop strategies to protect itself. For example, key threats facing the company are likely to be the growth and strength of competition, particularly supermarket "own brand" products. Opportunities could be linked to changes in consumer lifestyles, which might allow T to exploit the company's research and development competence in developing new product ranges. The outcomes from the corporate appraisal will provide T with an assessment of the strengths and weaknesses, opportunities and threats in relation to the internal and external factors and are often summarised in a SWOT.

Answers to questions 8-10 Project management

Question 8

Project management has nine key elements to it. The responsibilities of the project manager will be to manage each of these nine elements.

Scope
At the outset of the project, the project manager will define the scope of the project and set objectives. These will then need to be agreed with the Board of Directors before the project begins and form the basis for the overall project direction.

Risk management

The project manager will be responsible for identifying any major risks associated with the project (e.g. a supplier delivering late), and managing these risks through transferring risks to other parties, avoiding risks or accepting them and managing the consequences as they happen.

Integration

The project manager will need to develop plans for the development and implementation of the new systems. This will ensure that the process happens quickly and easily and uses the resources in the best way.

To integrate the new system into the organisation, these plans will need to consider change in management issues. People have been using the old system for some while and will need to adapt to the change in approach. It may also mean changing job roles and working practices which could cause conflict and staff dissatisfaction if not effectively managed.

Time

Each of the activities will need to be defined and their duration estimated. They can then be sequenced and time schedules made, using techniques such as Gantt charts or Network analysis. This will help to ensure the project is well organised and co-ordinated.

Cost

A budget for the project must be defined. This might be done through cost estimates from suppliers or by costing each specific element of the project individually. Throughout the course of the project, the project manager will need to monitor costs and take control action if costs are not in line with budget.

Quality

It is the project manager's responsibility to develop the Project Quality Plan which outlines expected quality of the new information and systems. They will need to monitor progress against this plan and ensure that the quality objectives are met. This will mean ensuring that the systems are developed by experienced suppliers and adequate testing is undertaken prior to the system going live.

Resources

This will involve the acquisition and effective management of staff, materials, buildings and equipment, and ensuring that each of these resources are adequately co-ordinated and managed.

Communication

Communication to all stakeholders will need to be undertaken on a regular basis. This will include reporting to the Board of Directors on progress, and agreeing any major changes in scope.

It will also involve good team communication and management to ensure team members remain motivated and committed to the project.

Procurement

The project manager will be responsible for procuring goods and services from external suppliers. This is likely to include the design and development of the new information system since ABC have little in-house expertise.

Question 9
The skills required by the project manager are as follows.

Change management skills
They will have to be skilled in understanding the people aspects of the change and helping to overcome resistance to change. This may involve knowledge of change management tools such as Lewin's force field analysis and Freeze/Move/Unfreeze model.

IT skills
Since the project is IT-based, some IT knowledge and ability will help the project manager to understand the key issues and negotiate effectively with suppliers.

Leadership
Leadership involves obtaining results through personal direction and influence. The project manager will need to be able to create a vision for their team, be assertive and inspire and motivate staff.

People skills
The project manager will need to understand the concerns and motivations of team members and to effectively manage them. This may involve the use of a suitable management style and understanding of approaches to the motivation of staff. The aim will be to create a motivated, happy team who work well to achieve the project's goals.

Communication skills
A key role of the project manager is communication, be that with staff, suppliers or the Board of Directors. They will therefore have to be able to use a variety of communication methods (presentations, meetings, reports, e-mails) and know when to use these appropriately and be skilled at using each.

Problem-solving and decision-making skills
There will inevitably be many decisions to be taken during the course of the project and problems to be overcome. The project manager needs to be an analytical thinker who will be able to solve problems as they arise and who is firm and decisive so that the project is not delayed.

Negotiation skills
Negotiation with suppliers and internal departments is an inevitable part of the process. The project manager will need to understand the basics of negotiation in order to ensure the best outcomes are achieved for ABC Ltd. This may involve being able to understanding leverage points over potential suppliers, being able to see the other parties' perspective and being firm and willing to walk away when the deal is not right.

Planning skills
The project manager will need project planning skills, and need to be able to use project management software to make and monitor plans. Knowledge of techniques such as Gantt charting and Network analysis will facilitate this process.

Some basic financial knowledge or expertise would be an asset to help with the budgeting and cost monitoring process.

Question 10

An objective is a target towards which the project is directed. In this instance an objective might include

- To have installed a new information system to meet the organisation's information needs within 12 months.

A good objective will have the following qualities.

Specific

The objective will be clearly stated so that it is clear what is trying to be achieved. In the example given "to meet the organisation's needs" could be made more specific by outlining some of the key elements that will mean that these needs will be met.

Measurable

A measurable objective allows the successful achievement of objectives to be assessed. This allows for performance to be measured which in turn helps to motivate staff. In the above example it will be difficult to measure whether the "organisation's needs" are met, so again more detail is required here. On the other hand, it will be very easy to measure whether the system has been installed within 12 months.

Achievable

An achievable objective ensures that the project manager and team will be motivated. When objectives are set which staff do not believe they can achieve, they get demoralised and soon give up on trying to achieve the target, making it worthless.

Relevant

The project objectives should be relevant to the scope of the project and the needs of the organisation and users from the project. This ensures that the project is focused on achieving the right aims.

Time bound

Without a clearly set time there is little motivation to work quickly and effectively. Deadlines focus people's actions and provide a clear point at which performance can be measured.

Objectives are important in project management for ABC for the following reasons.

Motivation

They provide clear targets to work towards which will motivate the project manager, team and suppliers. If there are incentives for achieving objectives, such as suppliers having to accept reduced payments if they do not achieve targets or team members receiving bonuses for hitting them, then motivation can be increased further.

Focus planning

Plans can be created based around the targets set. This allows for the best planning of resources for the project. It also allows for resources to be used to balance out the various objectives in the areas of cost, quality and time recognising that all are important and preventing focus on any one.

Allows for performance measurement

Performance can be measured against targets set, especially if intermediate objectives (or milestones) are created during the life of the project. This allows progress to be monitored and where necessary problems to be rectified. For example, if a time objective is not met, plans will need to be rearranged to speed work up, perhaps by allocating more resources to the limiting factor.

Question 11

The success of H Company's relocation project will depend, to some extent, on the effectiveness of the communication process between the different project stakeholders. The communication process model is a helpful framework that could be used to explain to P how to ensure that his communications about the relocation are more effective.

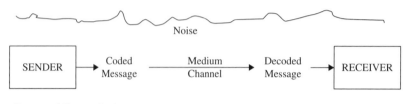

Process of Communication

Referring to the model above, it would seem that there are a number of barriers to effective communication in the relocation project, starting with P himself as the sender of the messages. The messages sent by P are too complex and often poorly expressed. They are not fully understood by the team members (receivers) because of the technical jargon P is using. He is also overloading them with e-mails that contain too many different issues, not all of which are relevant to the receiver. This could result in members of the project team not picking up the most important elements of the message that they need to act on.

To make communications more effective P should plan the communication. He needs to think about what is to be communicated, to whom it is to be communicated and the best medium to use for the message he wants to send. For instance should the message be communicated verbally or written, formal or informal etc?

P should define the purpose of the message with the receiver in mind and select the most appropriate language and medium for the message. He should think about the situation that the receiver will be in when the message is received. P needs to take care not to cause confusion in the communication process through the over use of jargon or lack of fluency of his message. In other words are communications being made needlessly complex?

P should have a clear objective in terms of what he wants to achieve from the communication. For example, is the communication aimed at providing information on the progress of the project for the project sponsor, or does it require specific actions to be taken by the project team. He then needs to code his messages in a way that is understood by his audience.

It is important that P's non-verbal communication reinforces his verbal messages and does not undermine them. If the medium channel P selects personal presentations, such as team briefings, he needs to ensure that all elements of communication, for instance words used tone and non-verbal signals (gestures, facial expressions, and posture) all fit with each other rather than contradict, so as not to confuse the receivers. P needs to anticipate possible reactions by the receivers to the message and cater for these through the message or choice of medium. For example if the message from P relates to bad news about the project this could upset the recipient and it might therefore be more appropriate to use face-to-face communications. P should also be aware of individual bias and selectivity by the receiver which occurs because often people hear and see what they want to. To help minimise this problem P should ensure that communication is two way, encouraging feedback from the receiver.

Feedback is often a neglected part of the communication process, but should provide a crucial check for P to ascertain if his message has been correctly understood and interpreted.

P also needs to be aware of 'noise' that can occur in the communication process. This refers to any distractions or interference in the environment in which the communication is taking place and which can impede the transmission of the message. It happens when the message becomes distorted by extraneous factors between P and the receiver of the message.

Distractions in the environment, information overload, the overuse of e-mails for complex messages are all examples of 'noise'. People can feel weighed down by the high volume of information that is being transmitted, and hence ignore the communication.

Question 12

Project completion is an important part of the project management lifecycle. Essentially it is about determining if the project has met X hotel chain's original requirements and the original project objectives. More importantly, have they been achieved in terms of cost, schedule and scope?

On completing the project, S should produce a project completion report. This involves client sign-off, which in this case would be done by the hotel chain for which the customer reservation system has been designed.

The completion report for the new customer reservation system should include a summary of the project outcomes, for example:

- Achievement of project deliverables and handover to the client, X hotel chain – that is. The design and implementation of the reservation system. Agreement with the customer that all deliverables have been provided successfully receiving and making any final payments associated with the project.
- The final budget showing the expected versus the actual expenditure.
- The time taken against the original schedule – that is was the project completed within six months and the reasons for any variances.

Another issue that should be considered during this stage is how any problems that arise after project completion should be addressed, for example who is responsible if any bugs in the customer reservations system occur once it has gone live. S should have tested out the system prior to sign-off to ensure that it is fit for purpose, but it is possible that glitches in the system could occur when it is used.

S should also undertake a post-completion audit which would include input from other members of the project team to obtain feedback on what went well, and why, and what didn't go well, and why. This is an important part of project management since it helps to identify lessons that may be learnt that could benefit S in running future projects.

The audit will examine the project in terms of:

- Did the project meet the client's expectations (that is did the customer reservations system meet X Hotel's expectations in terms of delivering its objectives on time and within budget?
- Was the management of the project successful – this provided S with the opportunity to learn how to manage future projects more effectively?

The information should be put together in a report including:

- A summary which covers where the project management organisation and tools have helped or hindered the project;

- A review of the end results of the project compared with the results expected highlighting any significant discrepancies, with suggestions on how any problems could be prevented in future projects;.
- Cost benefit review, comparing forecasted costs and benefits with actual costs and benefits – and identifying the reasons for over or under expenditure;
- Recommendation on steps which could be taken to improve the project management procedures used by S.

The post-completion report should be a useful document that S could refer to before starting any future projects that are of a similar nature.

Question 13

Project initiation is usually classed as the first stage of the project planning process and is an important stage in project management since it involves developing the initial project plans. It sets out the vision for the project and the establishment of goals and objectives. It is at this stage that the members of the project team will need to determine the scope and objectives of the project, undertaking feasibility analysis. The Project Initiation Document (PID) will be created which sets out the project success criteria.

The PID is sometimes referred to as the project charter, project brief or project authorisation document. The purpose of the PID is to provide a base document against which progress and change through the life of the project can be assessed. It will help in the school building project by setting out the initial project plans and defining the terms of reference for the project and ensuring that coordination and control systems for the project are in place.

The document will provide the background, for example, why the project is necessary, with some justification for rebuilding and equipping of the school as opposed to raising money for some other project in the earthquake zone.

An overview of the project in the PID will provide information on the key dates, the project objectives, specifying exactly what the project should deliver. The objectives can be defined in terms of the 'triple constraints of the time they should take, what they should cost and the quality that should be delivered. In this case the desired outcomes are the construction and equipping of a new school building in twelve months. Any constraints should also be acknowledged such as budget or available resources (that is people, money and equipment needed). Since fundraising is part of the project, the amount of funds that must be raised to fund the school project should be estimated.

The PID will help the project team to convey the scope of the project in terms of what is to be included and can be achieved by defining the principal deliverables. The document can be used so that the project team is in general agreement about the nature of the project. To avoid confusion and argument between people during the life of the project it will also be worth determining anything that is not included. Otherwise there is a danger that the project could get too big and out of hand as the volunteers think up other things they might want to do to help the disaster area.

Whilst the project team is made up of volunteers the PID should set out the roles, responsibilities and signatory powers of the different members during the project, along with other issues associated with control. The communications, types of meetings and reports should also be explained in the document.

Question 14

Corporate governance concerns the ownership and control of profit-making organisations and the relationship between owners and managers. A number of reports have been produced to address the risk and problems resulting from poor corporate governance. In the UK the most significant reports include the Cadbury, Hempel and Greenbury reports. The recommendations are merged into a Combined Code which comprises the purpose and principles of good corporate governance for listed companies.

There are a number of corporate governance issues facing Y Company particularly if it became listed on the stock exchange.

- It is problematic for one person to hold both the role of Chairman and Managing Director since this can result in too much concentration of power being in the hands of one person, and the greater dangers of the misuse or abuse of power. As illustrated in the scenario, it is difficult for other directors to challenge M's decisions. M, through his dominance and associated behaviours, combining chairperson and chief executive roles contravenes much of the recent thinking on corporate governance. This advocates that the separation of the two roles is essential for good control.
- It is evident from the scenario that Board meetings are ineffective, they are held on an irregular and infrequent basis with M wielding his power over other directors. It would seem that he has forced through decisions that are in his own personal interest and could be detrimental to the company. One of the core principles of the Combined Code is that listed companies should be led by effective Boards, which meet regularly and membership should be a balance of executive and non-executive directors so that no individuals or small groups can dominate decision making. It would be appropriate for non-executive directors to be appointed to the Board of Y Company to provide independent judgements on decisions.
- It seems that there is a lack of adequate control, accountability and audit in the company. The Board is responsible for presenting a balanced and understandable assessment of the company's financial position. It is responsible for maintaining a sound system for internal controls to safeguard the company's assets and shareholders' investment. Y Company should establish through an audit committee formal and transparent arrangements for considering how to apply the principles of financial reporting and internal control. Non executive directors should satisfy themselves on the integrity of financial information and that controls are robust.
- M has determined his own remuneration package, which he is keen to keep covered up. Good corporate governance practice states that no director should be involved in determining his/her own remuneration. Non executive directors should be responsible for determining a policy on the remuneration of executive directors and specific remuneration packages for each director, a proportion of which should be linked to corporate and individual performance. It is good practice to include a report on the remuneration policy for directors in the annual accounts.

The above points would help support the Finance Director who has been placed in an awkward situation regarding the questionable accounting practices and M's remuneration.

Ethical issues arise when one person's values conflict with those of others. M appears to be making decisions that are not within acceptable standards of honesty and integrity. In his position he should be setting the moral tone for Y Company, but in this case it seems that M is abusing his power. This is illustrated by M's lack of ethical behaviour regarding the acceptance of bribes, insider dealing, and the secret negotiations to move manufacturing to a country where workers could be exploited. Other members of the Board may have different ethical values regarding the potential exploitation of labour and the loss of jobs but seem to be unwilling or unable to challenge M.

Answers to questions 15–18 Management of relationships

Question 15 – Disciplinary procedure
In the UK, most organisational discipline is covered by the ACAS Code of Practice.

The ACAS Code of Practice specifies the requirements of good disciplinary procedures (e.g. they should be in writing; they should be non-discriminatory) and lays down how disciplinary incidents should be dealt with. The code states that for any incident the following applies:

- It should be thoroughly investigated and a written record made.
- A first warning should be given – this may either be oral or written.
- A final written warning should be given – this will warn of punitive action and explains appeal procedure. Formal warnings have a limited period of validity (e.g. 12 months).

Other recommended guidelines include:

- The worker should be given information which specifies the levels of management which have the authority to take the various forms of disciplinary action.
- Workers should be informed of the complaints against them and where possible all relevant evidence before any hearing.
- Workers should be provided with an opportunity to state their case before decisions are reached.
- Workers should be provided with the right to be accompanied.
- Management should ensure that, except for gross misconduct, no worker is dismissed for a first breach of discipline.
- Management should ensure that workers are given an explanation for any penalty imposed.
- A right of appeal should be provided – normally to a more senior manager. The procedures to be followed should be specified.

Question 16 – Tauranga
Disciplinary procedures
(a) Sean has a number of alternatives to dismissal and these include:

- *Reprimand* – an informal warning may be all that is needed
- *Job design* – changing the nature of the job
- *Incentive* – the assistant may be motivated by money
- *Training* – to improve job performance and possibly increase motivation
- *Transfer* – this may be difficult in such a small organisation
- *Support* – Sean should recognise that his assistant's problems may arise from outside the organisation.

Only as a final solution should Sean consider release.

(b) Many organisations will have a handbook outlining the steps which formal disciplinary processes must pass through. These are typically endorsed by the trade union. Once established they are legally binding.

Given that Tauranga is a relatively small organisation it is unlikely that it will have these in place. However, the following procedures should be adopted:

- interview the assistant in the presence of a representative
- produce a written account of meeting
- carry out a second interview in presence of representative with written warning of dismissal
- dismissal.

Question 17 – Take me to your leader

Leadership is the process of influencing others, to work willingly towards goals to the best of their capabilities, perhaps in a manner different to that which they would have otherwise chosen.

This question requires reference to any ONE well-known classification. As such the examiner is looking for an explanation of any ONE theorist. These would include:

Likert

Likert identified four styles of management:

1. *Exploitative authoritative* – Manager makes decision and enforces it.
2. *Benevolent authoritative* – Manager makes decision and sells it.
3. *Consultative* – Manager asks for suggestions on what he should decide.
4. *Participative* – Manager asks for solutions to problems.

Tannenbaum and Schmidt

They suggest that leadership style is a continuum from the Dictatorial to the *Laissez-faire*:

- Manager makes decision and tells.
- Manager sells decision.
- Manager presents ideas and invites questions.
- Manager presents tentative decisions subject to change.
- Manager presents problems, gets suggestions and makes decision.
- Manager defines limits, asks group to make decision.
- Manager permits subordinates to function within limits defined by superior.

Blake and Mouton

Two basic criteria for leadership:

1. concern for task (or production) being achieved
2. concern for people.

A high concern for the task will score 9 and a high concern for people will also score 9. Types of management:

- Task-orientated style (task = 9, people = 1 or 9, 1) – gets the job done but ignores peoples needs.
- The Country club style (1, 9) – attentive to peoples needs but ignores the task.
- The Impoverished style (1, 1) – ignores people's and task needs.
- The Middle Road (5, 5) – adequate attention to both needs.
- The Team style (9, 9) – gets the job done (task needs) and attentive to peoples needs.

Adair – action-centred leadership

Effective leadership style requires bringing together the needs of:

- *Task* – Objective setting, planning of tasks, allocation of responsibilities.
- *Team* – Team building, communication and discipline, acting as external representative.
- *Individual* – Coaching, counselling, motivation and development.

Fiedler

The most effective leadership style depends on the situation they find themselves. The situation can be defined by a combination of three factors:

1. leader and members relations
2. task structure
3. leader's power position.

Fiedler's conclusions were:

- A distant style is effective when situations are very favourable or unfavourable.
- A close style works best when the situations are not extreme.

Question 18 – The Northern College

Northern College is suffering from many internal and external conflict situations. If the situation continues it may lead to serious consequences.

The college is already failing to serve a sufficient number of students and the service is of a poor quality. Students and perhaps employers will detect worsening levels of service as employees stop co-operating to meet customer needs. This will lead to further funding cuts, targets that are more demanding, redundancies and more conflict between groups and departments.

While Northern College is experiencing difficulties, competitors who are pulling together internally could gain market share and suffer fewer setbacks. This could exacerbate the situation for the college and make it very difficult for them to recover their students even if the problems are resolved quickly.

The problems could lead to hostile and destructive behaviour by some employees. This hostility can lead to a number of problems. Notably poor communication – the withholding or distortion of information; interpersonal or intergroup friction; denigration of others; low morale and commitment; and annoying or disruptive behaviour.

Another consequence of conflict is that employees that are involved will be distracted from their work and suffer from stress. This could lead to under-performance and possible personal problems. Employees may decide to absent themselves from work, putting further strain on those that are left. As morale within the organisation sinks, key staff will consider leaving. This will lead to further morale problems, give rise to lost opportunities and lead to huge expenditure in recruitment and training.

Action by the trades union will worsen the company's capacity to compete. On top of the departmental rivalries, internal college cohesion will suffer further damage as the workforce clashes with the management. The management of the company could lose focus and direction as it becomes preoccupied with internal conflict and struggles to make optimal decisions as information stops flowing freely around the company.

Question 19

(a) Tuckman suggested workgroups (together with any other group) pass through four stages of development:

1. *Forming* – making a personal impression, getting to know the others, individuals may possibly drop out at this stage.
2. *Storming* – bargaining over goals, resulting in conflict.
3. *Norming* – developing agreed ways of working to achieve goals.
4. *Performing* – groups now begin to function smoothly and achieve its purpose.

The scenario suggests that the team is at the storming stage.

(b) Belbin made a long study of the mix of characteristics in a team. He concluded that a team composed of the brightest did not turn out to be the best (The Apollo Syndrome). An effective management team needs to have eight different roles (to which he later added another role):

1. *Chairman* – presides over the team and co-ordinates its efforts.
2. *Shaper* – the task leader.
3. *Plant* – the source of original ideas and proposals.
4. *Monitor evaluator* – dissects ideas and sees the flaws in arguments.
5. *Resource investigator* – brings new contacts, ideas and developments to the group.
6. *Company worker* – the practical organiser.
7. *Team worker* – holds the team together by being supportive.
8. *Finisher* – checks detail, worries about schedules and ensures that tasks are finished.

Later Belbin added:

Expert – technical person, if needed, to solve technical problems.

In the scenario it appears that Gordon recruited in his own likeness and employed people who might be categorised ad company workers.

Scenario-based answers

Scenario 1 – Strategic management (Answers to questions 20–22)

Question 20 – Tresco Insurance
(a) Cultural influences
Corporate culture is influenced by many factors which include

- the history of the firm
- its founder
- the structure of the firm
- the environment
- leadership and management style.

Each organisation may have a dominant corporate culture, but different departments may have their own.

There are many ways of describing culture and these include

Handy's "gods of management" focuses on organisation structure and practice. *Miles and Snow's* focuses on strategic decision-making (analysers, defenders, prospectors, reactors). *Hofstede* identified characteristics of culture which can be related to different countries.

Certain features may be seen as Cultural features within Tresco:

- *Strategic planning*. Tresco features a combination of defenders (defending their existing position) and analysers (moving into new areas if and when they open up). The change to a plc status throws all this open. The company is in a state of change – but too much of this seems to stem for a "reactor" mentality on behalf of senior management.

- *Values, beliefs and guiding principles.* As a mutual organisation, Tresco existed for its policyholders. The sales force were customer orientated to the extent that they maintained personal contact.

  The culture might have been based on, an ethos based on mutuality, rather than the satisfaction of demanding shareholders. The shareholders might demand wealth maximisation over the long term.

  However, as no single policyholder can exert control, the organisation may well have been run by management in their own interests. It is impossible to ascertain from the scenario whether the decision to mutualise and to become a public limited company was driven by the existing board. Significantly, no mission statement is provided.

- *Structure of the organisation and the type of work it does.* The branches where the personal sales force are sited featured a combination of two cultures.

  1. A power culture centred round the branch manager, who was supposed to inspire and control the sales force. The branch manager might be dominant and control the whole culture of the branch.
  2. A person culture in which people use the organisation to further their own goals. In the scenario it can be seen that salespeople who are independent and on commission were left to their own devices. Paid entirely by commission, some would have welcomed a low level of involvement.

(b) Changes in culture

The change in business strategy following mutualisation will have a profound effect on the culture of the organisation.

The mission of the firm may have changed from satisfying policyholders and employees to satisfying shareholders. The dominant stakeholders (key players) will now be the shareholders. The shareholders primary objective will be long-term wealth maximisation through the maximisation of profits at any given level of risk. The existing strategy and culture would have encouraged revenue maximisation with lax control over costs. Post de-mutualisation there will be a need for cost-cutting, which will change the culture of the organisation as a whole and the individual offices specifically.

The new management team has moved in this direction: whether it will develop from a reactor into an analyser or prospector (Miles and Snow) is not certain.

The change in ethos at the strategic level arguably replicated certain aspects of the salespeople's approach. The sales staff were paid entirely by commission, and were probably revenue maximisers. This will need to be a change to a profit orientation. However, the new salary structure, designed to enforce standards may be excessive. A greater commercial ethos at board level might meet with its dilution at the level of the sales force. There are other approaches to operationalising business ethics (e.g. codes of practice).

The newly expanded compliance department will promote certain aspects of a role culture. This influence is reflected in rules and procedures, and will be reinforced by the new salary-based reward system which is taking over from commission.

Not mentioned are the rituals and symbols of the firm. At times of change, some firms choose to embody these in a new mission statement – to communicate the emphasis on shareholder value – and a new corporate identity to indicate that the change has been made.

In summary, the firm will probably take on some of the functions of a bureaucracy (Handy's role culture). The business and strategy is more commercial and entrepreneurial – the directors are, of course, taking a risk by setting up a telesales operation when so many other firms have done so.

Question 21 – Rummidge Football Club (RFC)

(a) Any organisation has many stakeholders and all have their own views on what they are entitled to expect from the organisation. Stakeholders may be defined as "any group or individual who can affect, or is affected by, the performance of an organisation".

Stakeholders may be classified as falling into one of three categories. These include

1. *Internal stakeholders.* These are the human resource of the organisation and as such will comprise employees and managers.
2. *Connected stakeholders.* These are providers of finance and will include like share holders, providers of finance, customers and suppliers.
3. *External stakeholders.* These are any other group that has an interest in what the organisation does. It will include pressure groups, government and the community.

Stakeholders' interests:

1. *Internal stakeholders*

    Internal stakeholders of RFC include the club's directors, the club manager, the players, the ground staff and other employees such as those employed in sales, marketing, finance and administration.

    For internal stakeholders the relationship with the club is likely to be strong and long term. Both management and employees look to the club for their livelihood, for career development, for the opportunity to achieve something, for status and to associate with others. As well as guiding the affairs of the club, the directors are often major shareholders with a financial interest in its success.

    The players are key stakeholders because the club provides both their incomes and their careers.

    Managers and other employees will have a financial interest in the club and also have individual interests and goals such as:

    - security and maximisation of income
    - a safe and comfortable working environment
    - a sense of community
    - career development
    - a sense of doing something worthwhile.

2. *Connected stakeholders*

    Connected stakeholders include shareholders, sponsors, bankers, fans and their parents and suppliers. Like internal stakeholders, the relationship with the organisation may also be long term and strong but it is different. These stakeholders do not work directly for the club – although some may do as in the case of employees who hold shares – and so their concern is not with the day-to-day operations of the club as it is for the managers and employees.

    For the shareholders a major interest in the club is a return on their investment for a given level of risk.

Sponsors provide funds for football clubs as a way of showing their interest and also as a means of advertising. They are interested in the club because of the media interest when the team is successful.

Bankers who have provided loan finance will be interested in the club for both security on any loans granted and the interest they will receive.

Fans are customers and are interested in the club as a source of leisure interest and pleasure. Parents of younger fans are stakeholders as a result of their children's interest. As customers they buy the club's merchandise and have an interest in good quality products at reasonable prices.

Suppliers are interested in additional orders from the club and payment for what they supply.

The mass communication media such as TV and radio companies, newspapers and magazines have a financial interest because football is a game of worldwide interest and attracts millions of viewers, listeners and readers. For satellite-broadcasting corporations with specific rights to film the games, this provides direct income from pay-to-view charges and indirect income from the advertising income attracted by a wider TV audience.

3. *External stakeholders*

External stakeholder groups interested in the club include the government, local authorities, the community at large and the governing bodies in football.

The government and local authorities have an interest because they tax receipts from the games and the club's merchandise. The government has a duty to see the club complies with various aspects of legislation including health and safety.

The community at large and especially those near the stadium are interested from the point of view of parking, pollution, crime and crowd problems.

The football governing bodies are required by their constitutions to regulate the game and see that it is not brought into disrepute.

(b) All of the stakeholders will have an interest in the outcome of the bid for the club but the ones that are likely to influence the outcome will be those directly involved in the negotiations. These are the directors, the representatives of the satellite-broadcasting corporation and the football authority.

The directors are the legal representatives of the shareholders of the club. In many circumstances they will also be shareholders themselves. They have significant influence because they must recommend whether or not to accept a bid. The shareholders will determine whether or not the bid is accepted by voting in a ballot, but they are likely to follow the directors' advice.

The representatives of the satellite-broadcasting corporation are able to exert influence by how much they are prepared to offer for the club. As is often the case, the satellite company making the bid may not be the only interested party wanting to take over the club. There may be other companies waiting until negotiations start to find out how much is at stake; once this is known, better offers might be placed before the directors. Until this happens they are not key stakeholders in the situation.

The football authorities that regulate competition in the industry will also influence the decision. They will wish to promote competition in the industry and avoid over concentration of ownership.

Although they are not party to the negotiations, other stakeholders will have influence. The sponsors of the team may be direct competitors of the satellite-broadcasting corporation or may not agree with the principles involved and decide not to continue with their contract when it comes up for renewal. The supporters may try to influence the decision by exploiting media interest.

(c) Logical incrementalism involves the development of strategy using a series of small-scale changes. Plans are not made for the long term as in the rational model, but instead a series of short-term targets and plans are made to continuously move the organisation forward.

Such an approach:

- avoids conflict with stakeholders who are unlikely to oppose small changes to plans
- is flexible to small environmental changes
- does not allow for major changes, sometimes necessary for an organisation to maintain its competitiveness in rapidly changing markets. (The rational model is more likely to result in such a "revolutionary" change.)

Thus the directors are claiming that there has been little change in strategy and that which there has been has been evolutionary. Some of the stakeholders may not agree with this view.

Question 22 – Strategy approaches

The rational approach provides a step-by-step formal process to the development of a business strategy. It consists of a number of distinct stages:

(a) *Mission and objectives.* Defines the business purpose and direction.
(b) *Environmental analysis.* Examines factors external to the organisation, such as political and legal issues, the changing competitive environment and changing customer requirements to determine opportunities and threats.
(c) *Internal analysis.* An examination of the internal resources and competencies to determine the organisation's strengths and weaknesses.
(d) *Corporate appraisal.* A summary of the current position of the organisation, often using a SWOT analysis which summaries the organisation's strengths, weaknesses, opportunities and threats.
(e) *Option generation.* An analysis of possible strategies that will fill the gap between the current position and the future objectives.
(f) *Strategic evaluation and choice.* Evaluating options and deciding which ones to follow. This might include financial analysis such as NPV calculations.
(g) *Strategic implementation.* Putting the strategies into practice including polices and strategies for areas such as marketing, finance and R&D.
(h) *Review and control.* Evaluating the success of the strategy by measuring actual performance against objectives and taking control action by amending future strategies and objectives.

The rational model contrasts with the emergent strategies described by Mintzberg.

Mintzberg's research suggested that real world strategies often arise out of the course of business operations rather than from a formal planning process. Such strategies are called emergent strategies. Directors should be constantly aware of changes in the external environment and bring in new strategies and discard old ones which are not working as the environment changes.

Emergent strategies can be combined with the successful elements of the planned strategy to define the way forward for the business. The process of bringing these together is called *crafting a strategy.* This is more appropriate for businesses in a changing environment, where restriction to one planned strategy may be a competitive weakness.

Logical incrementalism involves the development of strategy using a series of small-scale changes. Plans are not made for the long term as in the rational model, but instead a series of short-term targets and plans are made to continuously move the organisation forward.

Such an approach:

- avoids conflict with stakeholders who are unlikely to oppose small changes to plans
- is flexible to small environmental changes
- does not allow for major changes, sometimes necessary for an organisation to maintain its competitiveness in rapidly changing markets. (The rational model is more likely to result in such a "revolutionary" change.)

Scenario 2 – Project management (Answers to questions 23–25)

Question 23

(a) Feasibility issues

The following key areas need to be addressed in the feasibility study for the website.

Business feasibility
Business feasibility aims to ensure that the website is consistent with the overall objectives of the games. A good website is likely to contribute to the stated objective of "level of customer enthusiasm and satisfaction", by providing access to information about the games to spectators and allowing them an easy method of buying tickets.

Economic feasibility
To ascertain its economic feasibility the cost of building and operating the website must be considered in comparison with the benefits obtained.

Costs will include

- building the website
- linking it to the information database to provide good quality information
- maintenance and updates
- costs of an ISP.

Some of the benefits are non-financial in terms of good quality information being provided to spectators and other interested parties. However some financially quantifiable benefits may also be considered such as cost savings through online booking in comparison to manual booking methods and additional bookings gained through online sales.

Social feasibility
Social feasibility concerns the way the project will impact people and the effects this will have on the project. Since there are currently few existing employees starting this project will have little impact internally besides the positive one of providing jobs. Website usage is also increasing in the general population which means there will be few barriers to prevent widespread access to the information, although to ensure everyone can access information and booking systems it is important that alternative methods are considered in addition to a website.

It is important the website is user-friendly, so using experienced designers and testing by potential users prior to it going live will help to ensure that it is well designed.

Technical feasibility

Technical feasibility considers whether the current level of technology is sufficient to ensure the project objectives are achieved. It also considers whether the project team to have the technical ability and know-how. Website development is now very common. The technical skills required should be able to be sourced with little difficulty.

One problem may be the volume of queries which the website will have to handle. It is likely that over the course of the few weeks prior to and during the games that visitor volumes will be very high. It will be important to ensure that the system specifications can cover this.

Due to the short timescale of the games it is imperative that the system does not breakdown during the games. Systems testing is therefore vital to the success of the website.

Operational feasibility

Operational feasibility concerns the way the website will work in practice and includes maintenance, information updates and allocation of people to undertake these tasks. It is likely that over the course of the games, extra employees will need to be contracted to update the site with new information. These people will also need an office in which to sit.

The main difficulty in this case will be obtaining resources (people and equipment) for such short periods of time. The best approach would therefore appear to be to contract out the service to an external provider.

(b) Activities of the project manager

The project manager must undertake the following key activities at the outset of each of the projects.

Project objectives defined

The objectives for the project are defined. This will include objectives for Time, Cost and Quality. These will be a guide towards which project plans can be made and act as the ultimate measure of success for the project team. This will ensure they remain focused on project objectives.

Fact finding and position analysis

Research will be undertaken to clarify project details, understand exactly what is required to be achieved and to assess potential problems. This may be through consultation with the FGCC and other stakeholders. Lessons may be able to be learnt from previous games through consultation with their project managers.

The results of the fact-finding exercise are summarised in a position analysis. This examines the project's Strengths and Weaknesses (internally within the project) and Opportunities and Threats (which come from factors external to the project).

Project activities clearly defined

The various options to take the project forward are brainstormed and analysed and the best approach clarified. A detailed analysis of project activities may be undertaken and included in a Work Breakdown Structure.

Project planning
Clear project plans should then be defined to ensure the project is well organised. This would include planning of costs (budgeting), quality and time (perhaps using a Gantt chart or Network plan).

Project approval
A business case will be prepared and approval from the FGCC obtained.

Team
The project team must be selected and their roles and responsibilities defined. The project team must be inducted into the group and their roles explained. A team meeting may also take place to engender good team spirit.

Resources obtained
Resources such as a budget, rooms, computers and so on must also be obtained and prepared in readiness for the project to begin.

Question 24
(a) Cost, time and quality trade-off

In all projects there is always a trade-off between the costs incurred, time spent and quality of final output.

As quality required increases, it is likely that costs incurred rise due to the higher specification, the need for better quality resources, better skilled staff and more experienced suppliers. Usually, this will also mean that the project will take longer as it becomes more complex.

In this case however, the Games must begin on the stipulated date (2 November 2006) even if quality of costs are adversely affected. This is because there are so many external stakeholders who will depend on this. This includes

- TV and radio companies
- Spectators
- Athletes
- Hotels.

For any of these stakeholders a delay is unacceptable, and whatever the quality of the games, it will very likely be deemed a failure.

This means that for the games, greater quality means greater costs as more and more resources are allocated within the limited timescale. Alternatively planning must begin early so there is sufficient time available.

(b) Time, cost and quality

Time dimension
Project planning. To ensure the project keeps to plan, the project manager must undertake detailed time planning. The use of Gantt charts or Network analysis will ensure that the project process is well organised and activities and people well co-ordinated. These project plans will need to be communicated to the various project teams to ensure that each individual part of the project is controlled and maintained within the bounds of the overall plan.

Uncertainty. In such a large project over such a long time period, there is always likely to be uncertainty. Such uncertainties can be allowed for using PERT (project evaluation and review technique), so that a reasonable time period is planned taking into account the inevitable problems that will occur.

Time monitoring. Progress against plans must be reviewed so progress is monitored. This allows remedial action to be taken in areas where the project is not keeping to time. Extra people might be allocated to these areas to allow progress to be speeded up. Project plans can be updated throughout the project to adapt to changes incurred and to ensure the project continues on track.

Quality dimension

Quality can be achieved as follows:

Project quality plan. The project quality plan outlines the expected quality of outputs and how quality will be achieved. Planning ensures the best use of resources to achieve expected quality levels. It also allows for the trade-off between cost, time and quality to be examined and planned to ensure that quality targets set are reasonable given the limited time and budget.

Quality targets. Setting targets for quality and then delegating these to key staff members ensure that staff are motivated to produce to the expected levels. For the games project this might include quality targets for each of the individual project teams.

Monitoring and controlling quality. By monitoring quality achieved as the project progresses, substandard work can be rectified. For example, if the website is tested and is found not to be able to handle the expected number of visitors to the site, hardware can be upgraded to allow for this.

Culture of quality. By setting an expectation in staff that high quality is the general norm through induction training programmes, communication programmes and by the leaders showing the way, a culture of quality can be developed which will ensure that all work undertaken is carried out to a high level.

Cost dimension

To ensure costs are kept to a minimum the following must be undertaken:

Budgeting. A clear budget must be set out for the project as a whole which outlines the total expected costs of the project. This budget can then be broken down activity by activity and allocated to individual project teams to use as a target for them to work towards. Budgetary targets allow people to plan within these limited means and keep people focused on costs throughout the project.

In the case of the games, there will be significant difficulties budgeting due to the one-off nature of the event and lack of experience in such a project previously. To make it more successful the following could be considered:

- Consult with committees who have previously hosted the games to ascertain the costs they incurred.
- Create a work breakdown structure, planning the detailed constituents of all activities to be undertaken, cost up each of these and add them together to get a total cost.
- Independent review by consultants.

Variance analysis. Actual costs can be measured and compared against budget on a periodic basis so they are monitored and do not get out of control. Where costs do exceed expectations, reasons for this can be ascertained and where possible remedial action taken.

Financing. Another key element of cost is to ensure that adequate funding is obtained at the project outset. This may be through commercial arrangements with sponsors and television companies, as well as through government funding.

Matching the funding with likely costs ensures that the games will be a success and ensure that expected quality levels are achieved.

Question 25

To: Farchester Games Coordination Committee

From: ZX Consultants

Date: 28 November 2004

Re: Farchester Games Project Planning

Introduction
In this report, the benefits of using a critical path analysis will be outlined and a critical path analysis produced so that the committee can understand its usage.

(a) Importance of critical path analysis

A critical path analysis is a project scheduling tool in which the project activities are recorded in a diagrammatic form. This allows:

- Critical activities to be identified. These are the activities that must be completed on time or the project as a whole will be delayed. Given the fact that the deadline cannot be moved in this case, it is vital that such activities are ascertained and closely monitored by the Project Director.

- The sequence of activities is clearly shown along with dependencies. For example, programming the communications system must follow analysis and design of this system. This will help you and the project director to plan activity timings and therefore plan when individual project teams should be set up or timings when contractors will agree to begin their work.

- The diagram can also be used for communication purposes, particularly to the individual project managers of project teams, who will be familiar with the format used, to ensure they are clear about the overall project plans.

(b) Critical path analysis

A critical path analysis is shown over the page. For the games project the total duration is 104 weeks, with the critical activities being B, D, F, I, J, K and L.

(c) Slack time

The slack time on activity H is 10 weeks.

Activity H can be delayed by up to 10 weeks and the project as a whole will still finish on time. This may help in the allocation of resources to the project. For example, fewer resources could be allocated to this activity (security arrangements and checks) so that it took longer, reallocating resources to critical activities.

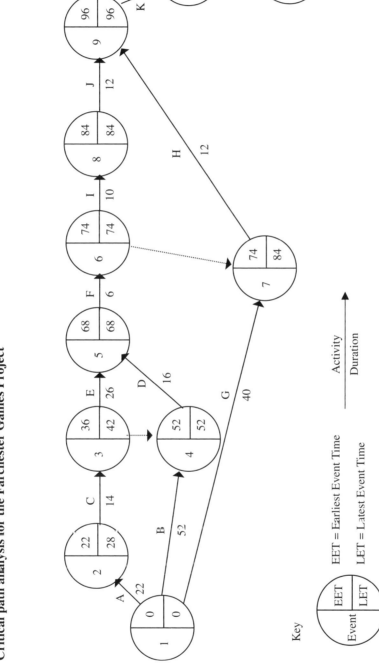

Critical path analysis for the Farchester Games Project

There is also some flexibility in the timing of this activity. It can start up to 10 weeks late and still not delay the project, so this can be used by the project manager in planning if necessary.

Scenario 3 – Management of relationships (Answers to questions 26–28)

Question 26 – CTC

(a) Vertical conflict occurs among groups at different levels in the vertical hierarchy. Horizontal conflict occurs between groups at the same level within the hierarchy. Many of the same concepts apply to both types of conflict but the groups and issues may be different.

The problem over pay differentials for mechanics is largely a vertical. It is a conflict between different levels in the hierarchy. It is a conflict between the management and labour.

However, there is probably an element of horizontal conflict between the two groups of workers themselves. That is, there is conflict between workers at the same level of the hierarchy. This may be based on their perceptions of their relative status and appropriate rewards.

The trade union is attempting to ensure more money for the mechanics. The underlying principle from which the Union might be working is that of equity and equality. That is, workers should be paid a fair wage for a fair day's work and workers should be paid the same for comparable work.

The dispute may arise for a number of reasons other than just pay differentials. Many studies have shown, it is common for workpeople to alienated; to believe that they have little power over their working lives, little status within the organisation and are generally exploited and treated with disdain at worst and indifference at best.

However, membership of a trade union who act on their behalf might give them a sense of collective importance and perhaps more importantly power. The power is as a result of the Union's power to disrupt the organisation's operations.

The dispute between the weavers and the inspectors may be seen to be rather more complex. It appears that this might have been initiated by the Works Manager's decision about improving quality, it is essentially a horizontal conflict between two work groups. There is a clear lack of goal congruence between these two departments.

The weavers want to maximise output whereas the inspectors are committed to high-quality output. Inevitably these conflicting objectives will spill over into personal relations. The weavers will see the inspectors as a block to their bonuses and the inspectors seeing the weavers as producing poor quality output in order to improve their take home pay.

The tasks of the two departments are interdependent; both deal with the same cloth, which must flow smoothly from one to the other; both make demands on the same machines, one to use them, the other to check them. Under these circumstances, a high degree of co-operation is necessary if conflict is to be avoided. The avoidance of negative conflict and its symptoms is one of the main functions of management.

(b) Resolution of conflict

There are a number of techniques that might be employed when conflict arises within an organisation. These are examined below in the context of CTC.

Avoidance. This is when one or more parties in conflict may seek to avoid, suppress or to ignore the conflict. This would not be appropriate for CTC as the conflicts are serious and any managerial inaction may lead to potentially catastrophic results.

Accommodation. This involves one party putting the others interests before their own. The management could aim to meet all parties demands. This will not be possible as management have the needs of a range of stakeholders to be met.

Compromise. Here each party gives up something. It is possible to recognise such things as productivity improvements without provoking industrial disputes. In the short term, the aim should be to resolve the conflict by negotiation. This would demand a willingness to make concessions on both sides, which may not exist.

Competition. This is a state where both parties do not co-operate and are encouraged to compete for any scarce resources. If the different workers were put in direct competition with each other it would appear to increase rather than decrease any conflict.

Collaboration. This is likely to be the optimum solution. Differences are confronted and jointly resolved, novel solutions are sought and a win-win outcome is achieved. This might be possible for CTC.

Use of power. If the industrial relations climate at the company is very bad (as it seems to be, judging by the threat of industrial action), it may be that the conflict will only be settled by a trial of strength. This would be no more than a short-term resolution, however, as the basic hostility would remain, ready to fuel future disputes.

Conclusion

Following the discussion above it might be seen that the best method to use is negotiation. Conflict resolution could be achieved if the reward policy of the company were to be changed to reflect the new, more complex goal. This could be done as part of the development of a new pay policy. It would be necessary to create a system that rewarded attention to both output and quality, but did not make it possible to achieve one at the expense of the other.

Factors influencing the likelihood of success

The chances of succeeding with either of these recommendations will depend generally on the extent to which the company is able to institute change.

The ability to change will depend on a number of other factors, including the skills of the managers concerned, the extent to which consultation and participation are allowed and encouraged and the external circumstances of the company. Change is easier when the organisation is under threat.

Given the current industrial relations climate at CTC, a proposal to abolish the inspection department would be highly provocative unless it were accompanied by undertakings about preserving employment and providing appropriate alternative opportunities. Such undertakings would have to be considered very carefully by management before they could be made.

There would also have to be a period of re-orientation and re-training before the new approach could be introduced. It is likely that this would have to apply all the way up the hierarchy. For example, if a production worker observed that a machine was producing unsatisfactory quality but had not actually stopped working, it would be appropriate for that person to halt production and summon maintenance assistance.

Managers would have to be able to live with such a degree of worker autonomy. This would be seen as a change in the culture of the organisation.

Question 27 – Helen Stoakley

(a) The examiner here is simply asking the student to set out an appropriate theory of leadership and then asking the student to pick one. The student should set out the advantages of that leadership style.

The leadership styles would include amongst others:

Likert

Likert identified four styles of management:

1. *Exploitative authoritative* – manager makes decision and enforces it
2. *Benevolent authoritative* – manager makes decision and sells it
3. *Consultative* – manager asks for suggestions on what he should decide
4. *Participative* – manager asks for solutions to problems.

Tannenbaum and Schmidt

They suggest that leadership style is a continuum from the Dictatorial to the

Laissez-Faire:

- Manager makes decision and tells.
- Manager sells decision.
- Manager presents ideas and invites questions.
- Manager presents tentative decisions subject to change.
- Manager presents problems, gets suggestions and makes decision.
- Manager defines limits, asks group to make decision.
- Manager permits subordinates to function within limits defined by superior.

Blake and Mouton

Two basic criteria for leadership:

1. concern for task (or production) being achieved
2. concern for people.

A high concern for the task will score 9 and a high concern for the people will also score 9.

Types of management:

- Task-orientated style (task — 9, people — 1 or 9, 1) – gets the job done but ignores people's needs.
- The Country club style (1, 9) – attentive to peoples needs but ignores the task.
- The Impoverished style (1,1) – ignores people's and task needs.
- The Middle road (5, 5) – adequate attention to both needs.
- The Team style (9, 9) – gets the job done (task needs) and attentive to peoples needs.

Adair – action-centred leadership

Effective leadership style requires bringing together the needs of;

- *Task* – objective setting, planning of tasks, allocation of responsibilities
- *Team* – team building, communication, discipline, acting as external representative
- *Individual* – coaching, counselling, motivation, development.

Fiedler

The most effective leadership style depends on the situation they find themselves. The situation can be defined by a combination of three factors:

1. leader and members relations
2. task structure
3. leader's power position.

Fiedler's conclusions were

- A distant style is effective when situations are very favourable or unfavourable.
- A close style works best when the situations are not extreme.

(b) The firm need to reduce the number of staff leaving the firm shortly after joining it. Methods of increasing staff retention should also increase morale and motivation within the organisation. Ways of reducing turnover may be seen under a number of headings:

Salary. Salary should be set at such a level that it is seen to be competitive with similar positions that individuals compare their roles. The complete remuneration package should be considered.

Appraisal. Well-structured appraisal systems should be in place. Employees need to know-how management assess them. A reward scheme may be attached to the appraisal system.

Training. Staff should be adequately trained to ensure that they have the requisite skills. Training has a number of further functions that will aid retention.

First, if adequate training is given it sends a signal to the trainee that they are valued. Secondly, a trainee is more likely to stay in apposition if they are receiving training.

Career progression. Most employees find it beneficial and motivating to have a clear career structure in place. If an employee knows that there is potential career progression within the organisation then this can serve as a motivating factor and in turn improve retention rates.

Social framework. Individuals seek much more than just money from work. Helen should ensure that thee is an adequate social network in place. This might be through social activities or even through the design of the office (e.g. break out areas).

Question 28

(a) According to Likert, there are a range of management styles:

1. *Exploitative authoritative* – where the manager makes decisions and enforces them taking no interest in their staff's welfare.
2. *Benevolent authoritative* – where the manager makes the decision and sells it, considering the impact on staff in the process.
3. *Consultative* – where the manager asks for suggestions from staff, but then makes the final decision.
4. *Participative* – where staff are given flexibility to make their own decisions with the manager's support and advice.

Robert Denney is in the later of these categories, the participative category. Robert is right to believe that this style of management is motivating to staff, since as Herzberg suggested, responsibility is a key motivator of staff.

However, studies have also shown that this participative style is not always the most productive. Staff can take too long making decisions and not enough time implementing them. They may have too little direction and support.

According to Charles Handy, the most appropriate management style is one which balances the following aspects:

(1) *Type of subordinate.* In Max Tools, subordinates are primarily lowly skilled workers. According to Macgregor, they would be deemed Theory X workers, who do not tend to want to take responsibility at work and need to be controlled and directed. This is at odds with Robert's management style and may explain why staff turn up for work late and take long breaks.

(2) *Nature of work.* Repetitive and boring tasks do not need much creativity, flexibility or skill. In this case a more exploitative style is appropriate, after all there is no need for staff to be changed in standard manufacturing processes. Indeed this may result in lowering quality as inconsistencies arise. Again Robert's style is not appropriate to the nature of work in the production department.

(3) *Nature of the environment.* Max Tools is in a stable industry which requires little change. Little flexibility is usually required for staff and their ideas for change are of low relevance.

On each of Handy's bases Robert's style is inconsistent with what would appear to be appropriate given the circumstances. I would suggest a Benevolent Authoritative style would be more appropriate to this organisation, where Robert takes most decisions, but does so in a way that maintains staff's general level of happiness.

Ultimately he must decide the most efficient and effective way to produce the products and staff should undertake production according to standard procedures.

This management style change will also require a change in structure, since there would be too many decisions for Robert to make alone. A functional structure would be more appropriate given the circumstances, with authority given to managers of each department to take key decisions in their area of expertise.

This style would involve Robert and his managers supervising staff more closely, and might include clocking staff in and out and only paying them for work actually done. This may help to avoid incidences of staff arriving for work late and taking long lunches.

(b) Scientific management was developed by Frederick Taylor as a way to achieve efficiencies in the workplace. Taylor believed in turning work into a science where each and every task could be analysed using work studies and the best way to undertake each task set out in a rule book. This results in standardised procedures that should be highly productive and produce high quality products.

Taylor did much of his work in a steel works where he managed to more than halve the numbers of staff required in by adopting scientific principles. As an example of the work he did, in one work study he calculated the spade size which would maximise the amount of coal that could be shovelled over the course of a day.

This approach is most appropriate in stable, unchanging industries like that Max Tools is in, since the procedures put in place do not have to be changed regularly.

In Max Tools, Robert could commission work studies of the manufacturing process to work out the most efficient and effective procedures. The manufacturing procedure could then be changed accordingly and procedures set out in a rules book for everyone to follow. This would be consistent with the benevolent exploitative management style suggested in part (a).

Set times for breaks and lunch could be implemented. This would be based on a mixture of legislative requirements and what was necessary to keep staff both happy and productive. This would reduce incidents of staff taking inappropriate time off work.

Taylor also believed in paying staff according to the output they produced rather than a set wage. He believed that people were primarily motivated by money and this method would encourage people to work hard. In today's working environment, this would be unusual and may result in staff dissatisfaction as well as making recruitment hard. It would also be restricted by the need to pay staff at least the minimum wage. However a low basic salary could be paid alongside a bonus scheme based on output levels to encourage staff to work harder and achieve targets.

Taylor also suggested that the most appropriate staff should be employed for a certain task and that staff should be trained in their work to maximise productivity. This would mean updating recruitment procedures so that clear criteria for staff for each role were set out and applicants reviewed against these criteria. Currently there is little staff training and a training programme designed around the new processes would indeed help staff to perform at their best.

Finally, Taylor felt that management should work closely with workers. Currently Robert's hands-off style has not been effective. Involving workers in the work studies to decide on the new processes would help to increase motivation once those were put in place.

Question 29

One of the most important steps for the project manager is to select an effective project team.

In the case of T's project, it will be a new team of people who have not worked together before, coming from different functional areas of J Company. To help the development of the team T needs to consider the manner in which the team comes together, since it cannot be assumed that members of the team will immediately work effectively together. To build an effective team it is necessary that it is allowed to progress through the developmental stages.

Tuckman describes a model of team formation which suggests that to be effective a team must progress through a number of stages, which have a linear relationship. It is only when these stages have been successfully passed through that the group can concentrate on the attainment of its purpose, in this case the design of the new range of educational toys, performing the project task.

The four stages identified by Tuckman are:

Forming: This is the initial period when the individual members of the project team come together, finding out about each others' attitudes, abilities and characters. The initial objectives and parameters of the team work are established which, in this case, will be determined by the project scope. It is at this stage that individuals will work out initial roles, and relationships, acceptable behaviours and codes of conduct.

Storming: This stage can be characterised as a period of disagreements, arguments and high emotion. As members of the team begin to work together and get to know each other, so they present their different views on the best way of achieving the project objectives and different approaches to working on the project. In the case of the new educational toys project individuals come from different backgrounds (e.g. marketing, production, finance, sales and IT) with different professional training and experience and will, therefore, probably have different views on what is important, hence conflict and hostility can emerge. This will cause the effectiveness of the team to fall.

Norming: It is important that conflicts at the storming stage are resolved. It is important that team members reach agreement over any issues through negotiation, compromise and finding areas of commonality. Team cohesion develops during this stage and norms of what is acceptable behaviour, which in turn, will govern individual members' behaviour whilst working on the project, are established. This stage is important in agreeing procedures and standards of performance.

Performing: When the group has successfully progressed through the three earlier stages it will have created cohesiveness to operate effectively as a team while working on the project. At this stage the team will finally be able to concentrate on the achievement of project objectives and it will be at its most effective because all energies are focused on the project task, rather than conflicts within the group.

There is a further stage, adjourning, which will happen when the toys project comes to an end, and project team members return to their normal duties. This is sometimes referred to as mourning, when the project team disbands.

T will need to use team building techniques to help shorten the forming, storming and norming stages and to motivate the team to perform effectively during the life of the project.

(b)

When the project is started, T, as the project manager, needs to get everyone working effectively together. However, there are a number of difficulties that can hinder the performance of a project team that T needs to be aware of and manage.

Blocks to team effectiveness can occur if the project objectives are unclear or are not accepted by members of the project team. This can lead to them working towards their own objectives, rather than the project objectives. In turn this can result in slippages to the project schedule and problems with project quality which could lead to cost escalations. If T is vague about the goals of the project or does not reinforce the importance of the goals on a regular basis this is likely to lead to a lack of team focus.

T must brief the project team on the overall objectives and goals of the project, and reinforce these throughout the project, using team briefings.

Another problem is that everyone on the project team may see the project in terms of their own particular discipline and background and may therefore have different opinions on the way in which the project work should be done. This could result in intra group conflict since people working in sales may have different attitudes and values to those working in finance. This can result in them going off in their own directions and lead to sub-optimising their solution of project problems. In addition, there may be personality problems between members which will arise if one member dislikes or distrusts another member.

T needs to be aware of these potential problems and take action when required. While recognising the contribution of the diversity of views and attitudes, T should, through team building activities, encourage ownership of project objectives by all team members. The overall objective of the project should be frequently stressed and the need to pull together as a team for the common purpose should be reiterated.

If T does not make clear to team members their roles in the project they may be unclear on how they are contributing to the project work and may feel that their lines of responsibility overlap with those of other team members. Team members may not know or understand what activities other team members are contributing or feel that there are no established procedures.

This could lead to conflict between team members. Individuals could withdraw into what they feel are their own areas of project responsibility and avoid co-operation and communication with other team members, all of which could have a negative impact on the performance of the project.

In addition, whilst staff come from different functional areas of J Company, T may not have had the opportunity to select members to the project team, instead having them foisted upon her. Hence, they may not have the required expertise or provide a balance of team roles as suggested by Belbin.

T needs to communicate to the team at the start of the project the roles and responsibilities of each team member and make sure individuals are clear on the specific role they are performing as part of the Toys project.

Poor leadership by T can create problems with team work. If she doesn't create an environment in which the team can feel free to contribute and feel accountable for their individual activities this could lead to a lack of commitment by team members. T should make sure the team has the necessary resources, but also set targets for the team and individual members. She should provide feedback on how the team is performing against the project deliverables.

While project meetings are important, if T arranges too many meetings they could get in the way of project progress. They could result in unproductive meetings that are full of conflict between team members, ending up being demoralising for individuals. T needs to plan the meetings as part of the overall project plan, and provide agendas so that team members know the purpose of the meeting in advance, and what they should be contributing. She should distribute minutes from the meetings, articulating the actions arising, and who is responsible for following up the actions.

Another problem T may face is conformity in the group. This is where an individual within the group is persuaded by members to agree with a decision which is wrong and the individual knows that it is wrong (sometimes referred to as group think). This could have disastrous consequences on the overall project with an incomplete assessment of problems, selective bias in processing information, and a failure to examine risks of preferred choices. T could help the team overcome group think by persuading individual team members to participate, encouraging divergent views from team members, and emphasising the importance of a carefully considered decision-making process.

Risky shift phenomenon is another problem T may encounter. This is the tendency of the group to take riskier decisions than would be taken by any individual member of the group. Again this could have a negative impact on the performance of the overall project. T should encourage the group to consider the implications of its decisions on the project and assess the acceptability of any associated risk.

176 Exam Practice Kit: Enterprise Management

Question 30

(a) A project needs to be managed through its lifecycle, applying appropriate project management methods and skills, in order to avoid/minimise potential problems that could lead to project failure.

A key part of the project management process involves defining clear objectives and setting realistic estimates in terms of budget and time and resources needed. Without this it is unlikely that an estimation of the baseline budget and project schedule can be constructed to present a realistic assessment of the time and funding required, and the resources needed for the successful execution of the Shopping Centre project. The outcome could be that the project ends up with unrealistic timescales and the different activities may not be sequenced logically, to make the most effective and efficient use of resources. This could also result in budget overspend and delays in various stages of the project. Ultimately the project may fail to be completed on time.

As part of the planning stage, feasibility studies should be undertaken, along with an assessment of the risks associated with the Shopping Centre project. If these critical dimensions are not understood, the project manager will not have the opportunity to identify potential problems and determine the actions needed to deal with them nor develop contingency plans.

Given the nature of the project, not undertaking social and environmental feasibility studies could lead to future problems and disruptions once construction starts for the Shopping Centre. For example, the impact on the local environment where the proposed Shopping Centre is to be built may not have been considered, and potential social issues in terms of whether the local community might object to the plans due to the disturbances during the building work.

If the project objectives are not clearly defined and scoped, this can make it more vulnerable to changing client specification. Whilst it is not unusual for client requirements to change during the life of a project, if the project is to come in on time and within budget then D needs to be aware of what is feasible. When the objectives are changed during the life of a project there is usually a significant impact on project success and it is important that D is made aware of the consequences.

It is at the early stages within the project that roles and responsibilities are defined for the project team. If they are not clearly defined this could lead to duplication of activities or activities missed. The result might be that members of the project team do not work effectively together, along with poor communications between the various stakeholders in the project. Finally it is at the planning stage that various control mechanisms would normally be put in place. Without developing an appropriate control system there is the strong possibility of poor cost control and overspend.

Effective planning can minimise the potential problems outlined above. In summary, D is putting the smooth running of the project at risk by wanting to remove some elements of the planning stage.

(b)

There are a number of different tools and techniques that G could use to assist him in planning the Shopping Centre project. For example:

- Work Breakdown Structure. This technique is a critical part of project planning involving an analysis of the work required to complete the Shopping Centre project. The activities in the project are broken down into manageable components, referred to as work packages. The process defines the activities that must be carried out for each work package. Each work package will have defined responsibilities and deliverables for the Shopping Centre project that G can delegate.

The analysis of activities for the Shopping Centre project can be undertaken at a number of levels, for example starting with the major phases then breaking them down into more detailed sub-activities. G would be able to develop a task list from the work breakdown structure to assist in planning, control and monitoring the various stages of the project. The work breakdown structure can, therefore, assist in identifying the people responsible for each activity or work package.

- Another widely used project planning tool is the Gantt Chart. This provides a visual way of illustrating the sequence of activities in a project. Complex project activities are converted into constituent tasks and a graphical and understandable picture is provided. Although it does not show dependencies and internal relationships, it is a helpful framework in the planning of construction projects, such as the Shopping Centre development. It will show the time taken for each activity and the resources required, hence can be used to monitor progress against the plan and assist project scheduling by planning the timescales for the project. It can also be used by G to communicate the responsibilities for tasks to the project team.
- A variation of the Gantt chart is the resource histogram which shows the resource requirement usage and availability against a timescale. This will help G in the scheduling and rescheduling of resources for the Shopping Centre project.
- Network analysis, sometimes referred to as critical path analysis, is an important technique in project planning, providing a diagram showing the sequence and dependencies between activities or deliverables on a project. Using a work breakdown structure, network analysis arranges each work package/task into a logical sequence and estimates the time to complete each. The outputs from the work breakdown structure analysis will help the identification of which tasks are dependent on others. Dependencies are critical to project planning. Simplistically this involves determining the sequence, that is if activity B can only begin when activity A is completed there is a dependency. For example planning permission must be sought for the Shopping Centre before construction work can commence. This is a crucial activity in project planning and the allocation of resources.

  Having identified dependencies it is then possible to calculate the critical path, which is the longest sequence of consecutive activities. It identifies those activities which, if delayed beyond the allotted time, would delay the completion of the Shopping Centre project and how much float time there is on other tasks. In other words, by how much certain activities could slip before there is an impact on the expected time completion for the Shopping Centre project. This then enables the minimum possible time to be determined, and can be helpful in identifying where there is some slack time available within the project plan for any unforeseen circumstances.

- Another project technique is PERT (project evaluation and review technique). This is a development on network analysis that G might find helpful in project planning. The technique is designed to account for uncertainty in the project lifecycle. Each activity in the project PERT uses three time estimates:
  - the optimistic time based on the duration the Shopping Centre project would take if conditions were ideal;
  - the most likely/probable duration if conditions were normal or as expected; and

- the pessimistic estimate which is the duration it would take if a number of things went wrong.

These estimates are then converted into a mean time and standard deviation which meant it is then possible to establish the duration of the Shopping Centre project using the expected times, but also to calculate a contingency time allowance.

Question 31

The underlying principles of the resource-based view (RBV) is that sustainable competitive advantage depends on an organisation's possession of unique resources or distinctive capabilities that cannot be easily replicated by its competitors. This view contends that internal resources are more important for a firm than external factors in creating and sustaining competitive advantage. The RBV emphasises developing or stretching internal capability and unique resources, hence it is sometimes referred to as the "inside out" approach to strategy.

The emphasis of the RBV is the possession of scarce resources and exploiting these in order to achieve competitive advantage. This means the identification of resources by C Chocolate Company that are better than those of its competitors and that superior competitive performance results from its use of internal resources and capabilities.

Resources include all assets, capabilities, organisational processes, information and knowledge controlled by a firm that enable it to create and pursue effective strategies. They are often classified into physical resources, human resources and organisational resources. Resources can relate to a particular raw material, for example in the case of C, high quality cocoa beans, or may take a less tangible form, such as the brand name. The critical factor is that they are the things which enable the organisation to both outperform competitors and are difficult to imitate.

Research on the RBV has focused on the characteristics of the advantage creating resources. Different researchers present different arguments in terms of what these characteristics should be. For example, Barney suggests that strategic resources must meet four criteria. These are they must be valuable; they must be rare; it must be difficult for other firms to imitate; there should not be freely available substitutes. The more a resource meets these criteria the stronger a firm's competitive advantage. The criteria proposed by Barney can be used to assess C Chocolate Company's resources.

Resources must be valuable, in other words they must be able to be used to exploit opportunities or minimise threats in the external environment. This could be considered to be the case for C Chocolate Company which is using its marketing capability and IT systems to collect information and respond quickly with new product choice to meet the needs of changing customer demand.

Resources must also be rare, in other words competitors must not be able to have them. It is plausible that the unique recipes could be considered to be rare and possibly access to raw materials, although this will be dependent on how easy it is for other chocolate producers to get hold of high quality cocoa beans.

Resources must also be difficult for competitors to obtain and not be easily duplicated (that is difficult to imitate). One way to achieve this can be through patents and trademarks, but the best protection is often through intangible relationships created between systems, skills and knowledge which are apparent in C Chocolate Company. The structure and architecture of the company could be viewed as a unique competitive resource, i.e. having the processes and structures in place that enable the company to quickly spot changing customer needs and develop new products. Also the experience, skills and knowledge of staff could be difficult to imitate.

Intangible resources and capabilities are more difficult to imitate and hence can be viewed as a more meaningful basis for strategic development and for sustainable competitive advantages.

C Chocolate Company's strong brand name would help in this context.

Finally it must be difficult for customers to find a substitute. In other words, resources are more likely to be competitive if they cannot be easily substituted. This would depend on how substitutes are defined, but it could be argued that there are readily available substitutes to chocolate products.

In conclusion, it could be considered that Chocolate Company is adopting a RBV to its strategic development. However, it does not meet all criteria in terms of its uniqueness of resources. Nevertheless, it is both the use of resources and the combination of linkages between value adding activities within the company that are hard to replicate.

(b)

CIMA's Official Terminology defines a value chain as *"the sequence of business activities by which, in the perspective of the end user, value is added to the products or services produced by an entity"*.

Michael Porter popularised the use of the value chain as an analytical tool to examine the relationship between the different activities of an organisation to determine where value is added. Linking these activities to the various approaches to strategic development, Porter's view is that resources should be arranged to enhance either least cost production strategies or facilitate differentiation strategies, for example through product quality and product innovation. In the case of C Chocolate Company, it would seem that it is using its resources to pursue a strategy of differentiation.

The value chain framework can be used by C Chocolate Company to establish the different value adding activities that are the basis of its strategic capability, and hence assist in understanding its internal strengths (and weaknesses), how well the organisation's resources are being used and where value is being added. Part of this would involve assessing whether the strengths of the company actually matter. In other words, do they provide value to the customer, and benchmarking against the competition.

The value chain is built up of primary and support or secondary value activities.

Primary activities are those that are directly related to the creation or delivery of the product or service and include inbound logistics, operations, outbound logistics, marketing and sales and service support. In the case of C Chocolate Company, operations must create value in terms of the production of handmade chocolates, but also marketing and sales in supporting and building the brand. Management of outbound logistics will be crucial to the web based company in making sure orders are received by the customer and delivery dates are met, otherwise this could seriously undermine the customer relationship.

Support activities are those which help to improve the effectiveness and efficiency of the primary activities. They include procurement, technology development, HRM and firm infrastructure.

For C Chocolate Company, procurement of the high quality cocoa beans is a critical activity. Technology development is imperative to the production of chocolates but also in supporting the main distribution channel, and sales and marketing activities. The company's HR function has a key role to play in developing policies to retain staff with the key skills, knowledge and experience.

Porter includes margin in the value chain framework to denote added value, that is the difference between total value and the collective cost of performing value activities. The ultimate value C Chocolate Company creates should be measured by the amount customers are willing to pay for its products above the cost of carrying out the value adding activities.

To conclude, resources are of no value unless they are used by C Chocolate Company to create value to the final consumer. It is, of course, how well C Chocolate Company manages the links between its value adding activities that can help to sustain competitive advantage.

Mock Exam and Solutions

Mock Exam and Solutions 14

Mock Exam Paper

> Section A: Five short answer questions   **(50 marks)**
>
> Section B: Two scenario questions   **(50 marks)**

 Section A

Answer all questions

10 marks each. Total of 50 marks.

Johnny Vegas

Johnny Vegas is the chief executive of W plc a diversified plc which among other activities manufactures washing machines and similar products. He has traditional views about the purpose of business in general and his own organisation in particular. Though he is frequently pressurised by a variety of groups and organisations that think he should run the organisation differently, he sticks to the view that the purpose of business is to maximise shareholder (and his own!) wealth.

Johnny's son Arthur is ambitious and keen to take over the CEO role. In his view W plc has a responsibility to a wider range of stakeholders.

Question 1

Recommend the stages Arthur should go through in determining the priority of the goals of W plc when he becomes Chief Executive.

(10 marks)

W plc are considering moving offices. A project team of 10 people has been allocated to this project. The move is planned for the 15th week of the project since they must be out of their old offices by the end of that week. The steps in the process have been outlined below along with the timing and number of people required at each stage:

Step number	Activity	Planned timing (weeks)	People required
1	Review current arrangements and discuss needs with staff	1–2	8
2	Design new office locations and positions and agree with staff	3–7	3
3	Prepare the building for the move	4–14	9
4	Undertake the move	15	15
5	Post move follow up and problem resolution	16–18	3

Question 2

Draw a resource histogram for the moving office project, outline any problems that the team may have with regard to project resourcing and outline a number of possible solutions.

(10 marks)

Management of relationships

In recent years, sales of washing machines by W plc have declined despite an increase in the general level of sales in the industry. Indeed in their domestic market where until 2000 they had the majority of the market, they only have 40% by sales volume.

In late 2000 Johnny called together the most senior directors from within the organisation and asked them to nominate individuals from their own departments for a team that would be charged with putting forward plans to the board of plc for relocation to the Far East. Johnny had seen many of his rivals undertake a similar exercise and successfully relocate in cheaper labour markets. Johnny (only half joking) called this team "The A Team".

The task group met once a month with individuals working on the project between meetings. By late 2000 the group had proved to be highly ineffective.

Question 3

Using appropriate theory explain possible reasons for the ineffectiveness of "The A Team".

(10 marks)

Aerospace
This scenario covers Questions 4 and 5

The T Aerospace Company is in the early stages of planning the development of its latest commercial jet, the 007. The aircraft industry is a fiercely competitive one, dominated by a few large global players who operate at the forefront of technology. In this industry, competitors quickly copy any advance in technology or new management technique that might provide them with a competitive edge. Some of the T Aerospace Company's competitors have adopted team working as a means of speeding up their development and production processes.

The T Aerospace Company is thus considering the adoption of team working in its operations, but some of the traditionalists in the company are doubtful. They are concerned that the benefits of work specialisation will be lost. Some of the managers have had negative experiences with team working and so have strong reservations about the proposed changes.

Question 4

Describe briefly the essential features of a team and identify the benefits that the T Aerospace Company can expect to gain from the adoption of team working.

(10 marks)

Question 5

Describe the difficulties that the company is likely to encounter in the management of its teams and recommend how it might overcome these.

(10 marks)

Section B

Answer both questions
25 marks each. Total of 50 marks.

Bandit Cycles

This scenario covers Questions 6 and 7

Bandit Cycles Limited assembles mountain bikes and related products, and retails them by mail order. The company was started by Sunil (a cycling enthusiast) and grew rapidly in the 1990s as mountain biking became popular as a leisure activity and competitive sport. Like many entrepreneurs, Sunil employed relatives and friends in the early days of the business and, even today, still prefers to employ people recommended by his own employees rather than go through any formal recruitment process. In fact, this is typical of the way the business is run. There is an absence of formal rules, systems and procedures. The organisation structure is flat, with Sunil making most of the decisions. Sunil's style of management means that relationships with employees are generally friendly and informal.

But everything is not going well. The company is experiencing a number of problems that are minor in themselves, but taken together are proving damaging to the company's performance. The most serious of these is the increasing number of returns from customers who are dissatisfied with bike assembly, missing parts or product quality. But there are other problems such as late deliveries, lost invoices, slow response to customer requests and complaints that, taken together, are having a negative impact on the company's profitability.

In the face of all these problems, Sunil has reluctantly hired a management consultant to conduct an investigation into the running of the business. The consultant's report has now been completed and the main recommendation involves the implementation of bureaucratic procedures. Sunil read the report with disbelief. He had always been led to believe that bureaucracy was something that produced inefficiency!

The company is considering undertaking a full review of the business structure, culture and management. A project manager has been appointed to lead this project and is suggesting the use of PRINCE 2 as a methodology to be used to run this project. The project manager comes from a government background and insists that this is the standard approach used to control their projects and will ensure the project is well controlled.

Question 6

(a) Explain why the adoption of the features of bureaucracy (such as those advocated by Weber) would assist Bandit Cycles to overcome its problems and improve its efficiency.

(15 marks)

(b) Explain why Sunil might be right to be suspicious of bureaucratic procedures as a solution to his problems.

(10 marks)

Question 7

(a) Critically appraise the use of PRINCE 2 to manage projects and assess its suitability in this case.

(12 marks)

(b) Outline the eight PRINCE 2 processes in the context of the project.

(13 marks)

Mock Exam Solutions

Solutions to Section A

Question 1

Arthur accepts the stakeholder view. He will therefore have the job of reconciling the varying stakeholder requirements when he takes over.

Arthur will attempt to balance different objectives of different stakeholders. Where those requirements conflict, he must set priorities. One process he might use is stakeholder mapping as proposed by Mendelow and subsequently adapted by Johnson and Scholes.

Mendelow's matrix helps to identify the relationships that should be built with different stakeholders. A stakeholder's position in the matrix depends on two factors:

(i) The power to influence the organisation, and affect its decision-making.

   A large customer may have significant power and the organisation will change products, prices, location of production facilities and so on to meet this customers needs. Small customers have far less power and their needs are unlikely to be prioritised.

(ii) The interest which the stakeholder has in the organisation.

   The greater the interest in the organisation the greater the level of communication that will be required with them. Many employees have little power, but good communication of plans is important to retain their loyalty and motivation.

The first stage of Arthur's management of his stakeholders would thus be to classify them according to these criteria.

The stakeholders could then be treated accordingly.

Key players. Arthur must ensure that his goals must be acceptable to them at the very least. An example would be a major customer.

Keep satisfied. Stakeholders here must be treated with care. While often passive, they are capable of affecting the organisation if they are not satisfied. Arthur must thus keep these stakeholders satisfied. Large institutional shareholders might fall into this quadrant.

Keep informed. Stakeholders in this segment do not have great ability to influence strategy, but their views can be important in influencing more powerful stakeholders, perhaps by lobbying. Arthur should therefore ensure that they are kept informed. Community representatives and charities might fall into this segment.

Minimal effort. Stakeholders in this segment may be ignored by Arthur as they have both low interest and low power.

The matrix can be used also in another way. It may be appropriate for Arthur to seek to reposition certain stakeholders and discourage others from repositioning themselves, depending on their attitudes.

Question 2

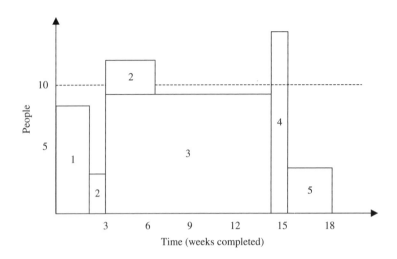

The project will be under-resourced in Weeks 4–7 (by 2 people) and Week 15 (by five-people).

Possible solutions include

- Aim to complete the majority of the needs analysis and design with three weeks to make use of the extra resource available in those weeks. Any finishing off activities can be completed by one person over the subsequent weeks.
- Using external contractors to undertake some of the work in the weeks where the project is under-resourced.

Question 3

There may be a number of reasons for the failure of the group to be effective:

Tuckman suggested workgroups (together with any other group) pass through four stages of development:

1. *Forming* – making a personal impression, getting to know the others, individuals may possibly drop out at this stage
2. *Storming* – bargaining over goals, resulting in conflict
3. *Norming* – developing agreed ways of working to achieve goals
4. *Performing* – groups now begin to function smoothly and achieve its purpose.

It may be that the group is still at the storming stage.

Johnny's team may well consist of the "best" people in the organisation.

Belbin made a long study of the mix of characteristics in a team. He concluded that a team composed of the brightest did not turn out to be the best (The so called Apollo Syndrome). An effective management team needs to have different roles which may not be present in this team.

Other reasons for the team being ineffective:

Ensuring a successful mix of roles within a team is vital but seldom achieved. This is due to

- lack of understanding
- lack of time
- people not available
- misunderstanding of task requirements.

Question 4

A team is a small number of people with complementary skills who are committed to a common purpose, performance goals and approach.

Team working allows work to be shared among a number of individuals, so it gets done faster without people losing sight of their whole tasks or having to co-ordinate their efforts through lengthy channels of communication.

A team may be called together temporarily, to achieve specific task objectives (project team), or may be more or less permanent, with responsibilities for a particular product, product group or stage of the production process (a product or process team).

There are two basic approaches to the organisation of team work:

Multi-disciplinary teams

Multi-disciplinary teams bring together individuals with different skills and specialisms. Team working of this kind encourages freer and faster communication between disciplines in the organisation.

Multi-skilled teams

A team may simply bring together a number of individuals who have several skills and can perform any of the group's tasks. These tasks can then be shared out in a more flexible way between group members, according to who is available and best placed to do a given job at the time it is required.

Team working offers a range of advantages. These are outlined below:

- It may increase a workers' awareness of the overall objectives and targets of a project.
- The various team members will work together hence the team will aid co-ordination.
- A team helps to generate solutions to problems, and suggestions for improvements, since a multi-disciplinary team has access to wider ideas. Ideally a team should have a range of roles in it – a fact highlighted by the work of Belbin.
- A team may improve work organisation. Teams combine the skills of different individuals and avoid complex communication between different business functions.
- Having teams may improve control. Fear of letting down the team can be a powerful motivator, hence teams can be used to control the performance and behaviour of individuals. This was seen in the Hawthorne experiments (Mayo).
- A team may result in less conflict. This is because the members of a team may have a greater understanding of each other.
- In addition a team may make conflict resolution quicker and more effective as communication channels between parties will already have been established.
- A team with a wide range of individuals may increase knowledge generation. Teams can be used to generate new ideas (e.g. brainstorming sessions (also known with more political correctness as "blue sky thinking" sessions)).

Question 5

Management theory such as that carried out by Mayo (The Hawthorne experiments) note many difficulties managing teams:

Conflict

Some theorists suggest that conflict is inevitable where human beings are concerned. A constant dedication to mutual support is simply unattainable and the potential advantages of team working are undermined as a result.

Group think

This is a consensus that not only stifles creativity but can also actually lead to a confident advance in quite the wrong direction. This is, perhaps, a special case of the common situation in which working in a team simply is not the best way to proceed. (President Kennedy was aware of this problem when he put together his crisis team during the Cuban Missile Crisis.)

The value of individuals

Some problems require individual flair and drive if a quick, workable solution is to be reached.

The role of the manager in team working

A common problem is the inability of the authoritarian manager even to understand the potential benefits of a more participative style, let alone implement it. The role of the manager in team working is not necessarily diminished but is changed to one of coaching and facilitating.

Solutions to these problems

Discipline and leadership

Subversive behaviour must be detected by close observation and tackled by a combination of discipline and leadership. This may take a long time, especially if the T Aerospace workforce has become disaffected by a history of bad treatment, real or perceived. Counselling and intergroup transfers may help.

Conflict between individuals can be tackled in the same way.

Group think and other types of poor performance are partly cultural problems and the remedy must come from the top. If innovation and drive are required they must be encouraged by example and appropriately rewarded. There must be some freedom to fail, where possible and appropriate. An aerospace company may have a particular problem here, with its over-riding need for reliability in its products.

The main problem T Aerospace will have will be with its managers. They will have to implement all these improvements and do it in a new and unfamiliar way. The company will find it necessary to provide extensive training for its managers and may have to recruit some new ones.

Solutions to Section B

Question 6

(a) Many of Bandit Cycles problems could be solved by the application of an understanding of the principles of bureaucracy.

Weber's description of bureaucratic methods offers several possible solutions. The elements of the bureaucracy together with how they might be used to overcome the problems faced by Bandit Cycles and how they might improve efficiency.

Hierarchy

A hierarchy is a series of offices, in which offices are linked through a clear chain of command.

Sunil makes most of the decisions at the moment. This may have something to do with his current problems, in that he is too busy to give proper attention to all the demands made on his time.

It may appropriate for Sunil to think hard about appointing one or more subordinate managers who he could trust to take responsibility for some aspects of operations and the less important decisions.

Specialisation – clear division of labour

There is a high degree of specialisation of labour. Employment is based on ability, not personal loyalty. It may be that some of Sunil's current problems occur because he is employing the wrong people, or because, while the people are potentially competent, they do not have the proper training, supervision and experience to get things right. Specialisation will improve productivity as specialists will be used in every function. For example, accounts preparation or drafting employment contracts.

Rules – strict rules and procedures

If there were clear rules set out then Sunil would not have to make all the decisions himself and would greatly speed the process of decision-making.

Impersonality

If Sunil employed the process of objective and rational decisions rather than personal preferences then the quality of decision-making should improve together with the organisations efficiency.

Appointed officials

Managers should be selected by qualification, education or training. Again the quality of decision-making should improve together with the organisations efficiency.

Sunil's appointments should be on the grounds of competence not personal preference.

(b) The idea of bureaucracy is often associated with negatives. Indeed the very word bureaucracy is often used in common parlance to indicate an organisation that is inefficient and ineffective.

Bureaucracy may have a number of problems and these problems arise for a number of reasons.

When profit and commercial survival need not be considered because political motives guarantee the continuance of the organisation, there is no external check on the proliferation of unnecessary procedure, hierarchy and so on

To this end, discretion is removed and decisions must be made in strict conformity to established precedent. Many decisions will have to be referred upwards through layers of hierarchy, with consequent loss of time and distortion in transmission. The organisation moves slowly and responds poorly to changing circumstances.

One of the main weaknesses of Bureaucracy is that it is not very good at dealing with an environment that changes very rapidly or in important ways. That is, there is considerable environmental turbulence. A bureaucracy may take too long to reach suitable conclusions about what the proper course of action is and its decision-making capability may be overwhelmed. In the public sector the organisation may survive. However in Sunil's case such poor responsiveness may be fatal.

In Sunil's organisation, for example, customer complaints are a problem. In a bureaucracy rules predominate. However, it would be very difficult to establish procedures to deal with all the variations of problems that might arise.

It would be far better to allow a responsible customer services officer to make an appropriate response within general cost guidelines. The guidelines would represent the full extent of the application of the bureaucratic method in this instance.

The challenge for Sunil and Bandit Cycles is to try and benefit from the best aspects of Bureaucratic management with not allowing itself to suffer from the problems outlined above.

Question 7

(a) Critically appraise PRINCE 2

Indeed, the motivation becomes one of proving that exhaustive consideration has been given to all angles on a problem and that mistakes have not been made. This encourages a defensive culture and rigid adherence to the rules.

PRINCE 2 is a standardised approach to project management process. PRINCE stands for "PRojects IN Controlled Environments". It is used by the UK Government and many private companies to organise and manage projects.

Advantages

Advantages of using PRINCE 2 to manage the project include

Tried and trusted approach

PRINCE 2 has been used in many projects and has been refined in its use over that time. This has ensured that it is a trustworthy and reliable approach to manage projects which includes many of the elements required to ensure the project is a success.

The use of PRINCE 2 will also give stakeholders external to the project (e.g. The Board of Directors, Shareholders) confidence that the project will be well managed and controlled.

Good documentation

The documentation required is specified in PRINCE 2. This includes production of planning documents, reporting requirements, an issue log, quality log and lessons learnt report. This ensures that project process is fully documented and helps to control the project.

Clear team structure and roles and responsibilities

The roles and responsibilities of the various parties such as the project board and project manager are clearly stated under PRINCE 2. This helps to avoid conflict and ensures various parties work well together. It also clearly defines the relationship between them (e.g. reporting required, authorisation levels) which ensures the relationship is clear and productive.

Familiar to the project manager

Since this approach is familiar to the project manager it should ensure that he/she is able to operate this approach effectively.

Familiar to project team

Many project team members will have had previous experience of project management under PRINCE 2 because of its popularity. This will ensure they get up to speed quickly and know the requirements.

Disadvantages

There will be also some drawbacks to using PRINCE 2 as a project management approach.

Project initiation and feasibility not considered

PRINCE 2 starts after the project's initiation, project feasibility and options generation stages of the project life cycle. It takes the view that the go ahead has been agreed and that the project now needs organising and controlling. In this case it does appear that the project has been agreed already, but it is important to ensure that earlier project stages are fully considered for completeness purposes.

Complicated and time consuming

PRINCE 2 includes many processes and stages which mean that a significant amount of time is spent on control of the project and reporting. This may mean that unnecessary time is spent managing and documenting the project causing significant delay.

Bureaucratic process

Since PRINCE 2 is clearly defined and well controlled the culture of the project team may become bureaucratic. Documentation and control may take precedence over innovation and flexibility.

Conclusion

On balance, PRINCE 2 would appear to be good approach to managing this project which will ensure the project is well controlled and documented.

(b) PRINCE 2 processes

PRINCE 2 has eight processes which require managing. These are as follows.

1. *Starting up a project (SU)*

   In this process a project board and project manager are appointed and a team structure designed. This will include defining the roles and responsibilities of the team members. A project brief is then outlined which summarises the project's purpose, key risks, objectives and approach. It also includes and initial Business Case which provides justification for the project. Starting up the project is intended to be of short duration. A plan for the next stage of the process is also prepared and summarised in the initiation stage plan.

2. *Initiating the project*

   Detailed planning of the project is then undertaken. This will include the production of planning documentation using Gantt charts and Network charts. It also means splitting the project up into stages and setting milestones to be achieved at each of these stages. Project files are set up including a quality log, lessons learned report and issue log. The output of this stage is a *project initiation document*, which unlike the business case does not change. It is a detailed project plan, with clear objectives, against which project progress is measured.

3. *Directing a project*

   This is the role of the project board. The project manager will report to the board who will

   - authorise the project to go ahead
   - authorise stage plans as the project progresses
   - give ad hoc direction (e.g. where problems occur) and authorise changes to plans
   - confirm project closure.

4. *Controlling a stage*

   Projects are divided into manageable stages to ensure the project remains well controlled. The number of stages will depend on the size of the project and the level of risk. Each project stage must be completed before starting the next and each new stage is planned in the preceding stage. It is managed by the project manager. Controlling a stage includes

   - assessing progress
   - capturing and examining key issues, and taking corrective action
   - reporting highlights to the project board
   - checking the output matches the product description.

5. *Managing project delivery*

   All outputs from a project are called products. The project manager clearly specifies products and manages their production and delivery by the team or external suppliers.

6. *Managing stage boundaries*

   At the end of each stage the project's progress will be reviewed. Lessons are learnt and incorporated into the next stage. Managing stage boundaries includes

   - updating the overall project plan
   - updating the business case
   - updating the risk log
   - producing an exception plan (caused by the project not meeting planned costs, quality targets or time plans)
   - reporting stage end to the board who authorise the project to progress to the next stage
   - planning the next stage.

7. *Closing a project*

   Closing the project ensures a clear end to the project, which prevents the project drifting into operational management, and provides an opportunity to celebrate achievement and learn lessons for future projects. Closing a project involves

   - agreeing with customers and suppliers that the project is completed
   - notifying stakeholders of project completion
   - formal handover of "products" to client
   - document follow-action recommendations
   - plan the Post Project Review (which evaluates the benefits outlined in the business case, the quality of management and identifies the lessons learnt)
   - conduct the Post Project Review.

8. *Planning*

   Planning occurs throughout the project, and is a constituent of many other processes as well as being defined as a process in its own right. Planning includes

   - defining the product and writing a product description
   - identifying activities and dependencies
   - estimating (timescales, costs, capabilities)
   - scheduling (what and when)
   - analysing risks and making contingency plans
   - completing a plan – including authorisation of the plan by the board.

Exam Q & As

At the time of publication there are no exam Q & As available for the 2010 syllabus. However, the latest specimen exam papers are available on the CIMA website.
Actual exam Q & As will be available free of charge to CIMA students on the CIMA website from summer 2010 onwards.